Scotland's Grand Slam '84

Scotland's Grand Slam '84

IAN MCLAUCHLAN AND CHRIS REA

Stanley Paul

London Melbourne Sydney Auckland Johannesburg

Stanley Paul & Co. Ltd
An imprint of the Hutchinson Publishing Group
17–21 Conway Street, London W1P 6JD

Hutchinson Publishing Group (Australia) Pty Ltd
PO Box 496, 16–22 Church Street, Hawthorne,
Melbourne, Victoria 3122
PO Box 151, Broadway, New South Wales 2007

Hutchinson Group (NZ) Ltd
32–34 View Road, PO Box 40–086, Glenfield,
Auckland 10

Hutchinson Group (SA) Pty Ltd
PO Box 337, Bergvlei 2012, South Africa

First published 1984

© Ian McLauchlan and Chris Rea 1984

Phototypeset by Wyvern Typesetting Limited, Bristol

Printed and bound in Great Britain by
Butler & Tanner Ltd, Frome and London

British Library Cataloguing in Publication Data

McLauchlan, Ian
    Scotland's grand slam '84.
    1. Rugby football—Scotland
    I. Title   II. Rea, Chris
    796.33′3′09411   GV945.9.G7

ISBN 0 09 159210 0

Contents

Photographic acknowledgement

For permission to reproduce copyright photographs, the authors and publishers would like to thank Colorsport, Associated Sports Photography, *Scottish Daily Record* and *The Scotsman*

Chris Rea acknowledges the help given by his newspaper, *The Scotsman*, in the research required for this book

Foreword

Having experienced the high pleasure of sharing in the BBC Television coverage of every one of Scotland's Grand Slam matches in the 1984 International Championship, I applaud the production, in the written word, of this fascinating study of the build-up and step-by-step progress to such a rare and historic Scottish Rugby achievement.

All the great milestones of history have their permanent written record and no one can deny the right of Scotland's 1984 Grand Slam squad to their place in the annals. Some will argue that they beat a Welsh side short of Terry Holmes and their best front row, that they caught an England lacking sharpness and fitness, that Ireland erred in giving them first use of the strong wind and that the French should have been out of sight by halftime but threw the game away by their lack of discipline and control. Like all successful sides, Scotland did enjoy at times that essential element of good fortune; but that apart, the team proved a superbly fit and well-organized combination. Their pre-match analyses were generally sound, they knew their strength and played to it and were able to call on marvellous resilience, dogged resolve and admirable *esprit-de-corps*.

It seems entirely fitting that the dramatic events and sterling qualities of this Grand Slam campaign should be chronicled in this handsome addition to the literature of the Rugby Union game by two of Scotland's most kenspeckle post-war internationalists. For Chris Rea and Ian McLauchlan each experienced the humps and hollows of Rugby at all its levels and are thus eminently well equipped, with the right instinct, knowledge and 'feel', to make an analytical assessment and record of a magnificent Scottish effort and of the failure of the other Championship countries to halt their progress.

Nor is it surprising that the root of their story is to be found in New Zealand 1983. As British Lions themselves, they appreciated perhaps earlier than most that although the 1983 Lions tour of New Zealand proved disappointing in several respects, it had a significant influence on its Scottish members and their subsequent Grand Slam success.

For me, the special highlight of that Grand Slam journey was the scintillating try scored by Scottish full back Peter Dods, as the final flourish to the game against Ireland at Lansdowne Road and the winning of the Triple Crown. It brought to fruition a sizzling handling move, cleverly created and beautifully executed, that involved almost the entire Scottish back division – the jewel in the crown, indeed.

That is just one of the many dramatic incidents related within these pages; in years to come they will serve as a permanent reminder of one of the most thrilling, proud and joyous passages in the history of the Scottish game.

Bill McLaren

1 The Long Bleak Summer

Midway through the 1983 Lions Tour of New Zealand, Willie John McBride and Jim Telfer, team manager and coach respectively, stood their ground, encircled and massively outnumbered, by a press corps which, if not exactly hostile, was in no mood for platitudes. It was reminiscent of a scene from an old western with the homesteaders grouped together in a tiny knot defending the honour of their families and preparing to fight for their lives against whooping Indians.

By this stage of the tour it had seeped through to even the most obstinate consciousness that the Lions were in dire straits. One wheel was all that remained on the tour wagon and the scalpels were out. But Telfer stood his ground defiantly. 'I am not,' he insisted, 'a loser.' Throughout the tour Telfer had impressed everyone as an honest, forthright man but even his most ardent supporters construed this boast as whistling in the dark. The Lions had already lost the First Test, failing dismally to take advantage of a temporary malfunction in the All Blacks' machine, and were on the brink of the biggest hiding in their history. It seemed certain that the careers of Telfer, McBride and the captain Ciaran Fitzgerald would be seriously, if not irreparably, damaged.

Telfer had made mistakes; he knew that and was quite prepared to admit to them. Mistake number one had been his belief that he could convert players from four countries to his way of thinking and that he could mould them into a team capable of playing and beating the All Blacks at their own game. For that he needed athletic, mobile forwards, and backs who were, above all, skilled craftsmen. Instead, the Lions arrived in New Zealand with a number of forwards who were as supple as teak elephants, and every bit as cumbersome. For them the ruck was the most evil creation devised by man and in the early stages of the tour, when Telfer was putting his reluctant charges through the simulated rucking exercises, it was incredible that no one was seriously injured. Regrettably, the haphazard selection was not confined to the forwards. One centre could run, one could pass, one frequently gave the impression of being able to do neither and one had been so badly crocked earlier in the season that he was in no state, physically or mentally, to survive the rigours of a major tour to New Zealand.

There were other reasons, of course, for the Lions' failure. One was the inordinately high casualty rate. Six replacements were required at various stages of the tour and seven players were unfit for service by the end. The severity of the itinerary, often criticized by McBride, was another major factor; how it ever came to be accepted by the Four Home Union remains a mystery. Before the First Test at Christchurch, the Lions were asked to play four of their six matches against first division opponents. Two of these, Auckland, the national provincial champions, and Wellington, the champions the previous year, were given midweek status; at a crucial stage later in the tour, Canterbury, arguably the strongest of the New Zealand provincial sides, was also given this status. McBride's criticisms of the itinerary were entirely valid, but less so were his occasional outbursts about the standard of

Jim Pollock equalizes against New Zealand. Pokere (13) looks daggers

refereeing and the behaviour of some of the Lions' opponents. The most senseless act of brutality on the tour was perpetrated, not by a New Zealander but by a Lion, yet not a word of condemnation was heard from the tourists' camp on that occasion.

One of the principal reasons for the Lions' defeat and ultimate annihilation lay in the grave misjudgements made by the selectors. Too often in the past had the Lions' selectors failed to identify the potential disaster areas in the domestic season and, by turning a blind eye to the Welsh mastery over Ireland at Cardiff, the selectors in 1983 were every bit as guilty of negligence as some of their predecessors had been. They chose to disregard the overwhelming evidence that the carpet on which Ireland had been flying for two seasons had lost some of its magic. It was true that Ollie Campbell had played majestically in Ireland's Triple Crown success in 1982 and, by breaking all scoring records the following season, had fortified an ailing Irish side. His 21 points in the final international of the season against

England had enabled them to gain a share of the championship with France. But to many observers at Lansdowne Road that day, Ireland's victory merely emphasized the extent of England's decline.

Much more significant was the 23–9 defeat of Ireland by Wales two weeks previously. Fergus Slattery and Moss Keane had given a typically rugged performance – but neither was going to New Zealand. The rest offered only token resistance to an enthusiastic but inexperienced Welsh XV and even Campbell had shown signs of stress. Despite this, eight of the Irish side won Lions selection that day and, although Lenihan dropped out before the tourists departed, both he and Ginger McLoughlin later joined the party as replacements. England, whose draw against Wales at Cardiff had spared them the humiliation of the whitewash, had contributed ten players to the party by the end of the tour, Wales nine and Scotland eight.

Scotland's best performance of the season had been, not at Twickenham where they beat a dispirited and disorganized England, but in Paris where they lost to France. The Scottish back row of David Leslie, Jim Calder and John Beattie had played superbly, the latter containing Joinel at the line-out and the two flankers laying the foundation of what was to be Scotland's *annus mirabilis* the following season. But not one Lions' selector was in Paris to see Scotland that day.

So, despite the incontrovertible evidence, the selectors left Leslie at home and Jock Hobbs, the successor to Graham Mourie as the All Blacks open side flanker, romped unchallenged around the paddocks of New Zealand. But Calder went and, after a slow start, prospered until injury kept him out of the side for the Fourth Test. Beattie was taken as one number 8, Iain Paxton as the other; it was Paxton who emerged as first choice for the Test side. This was in contrast to his fortunes during the domestic season when he had been kept out of the Scottish side by Beattie. Two other Scottish forwards were chosen: Iain Milne at tight head and Colin Deans, whose position as second string hooker was assured when Ciaran Fitzgerald was selected as captain. The refusal of the Lions' selectors to play Deans in a Test match was at the time, and for many months afterwards,

David Leslie holds the floor at a gathering of the clans

the subject of passionate debate; by his display against the Frenchman Dintrans at Murrayfield last season, Deans proved beyond all reasonable doubt that he has no peer either in the twilight world of hooking or in the tight loose. Ironically when the Lions' selectors had sat down to choose the thirty players for the tour, Deans was one of the first on the list. Milne was not alone in believing that he was worth his place in the Test side. Graham Price, magnificent prop though he was and notwithstanding his tremendous experience, was not the fearsome adversary that he had been in 1977 in New Zealand or in South Africa three years later. He was, however, spritely enough and wily enough to catch the eye in the loose with a regularity, which eased the doubts about his scrummaging.

There were three Scottish backs in the party: both half backs, Roy Laidlaw and John Rutherford; and Roger Baird who, as the one specialist left wing, had only to escape injury to be certain of a Test place. Alert and eager, Baird unfortunately came at the end of one of the slowest conveyor belts in Lions history; only once in the series – during the Third Test on a waterlogged pitch at gloomy Carisbrook – was he given a sniff of a chance. And he took it. The result was one of the two tries scored by the Lions in the Test series. The other was coincidentally scored by a fellow Scotsman, Rutherford, and in that same test match at Dunedin. Rutherford had been selected as a stand-off, the general assumption being that he would be Campbell's understudy. But, as the days passed and the three-quarters ran through their apparently endless repertoire of mistakes, it became clear that a footballer of Rutherford's class was too valuable to be left on the sidelines. Rutherford had gone to New Zealand, as so many other Scots before him who had been given the ultimate accolade of Lions selection, with a strong sense of inadequacy. He approached the first training session convinced that his imaginary shortcomings were about to be exposed but, by the end of the first week, he knew that he had

nothing to fear. On the contrary, he was surprised and not a little alarmed to discover how unskilled many of his travelling companions were.

Had there been a prize for valour on the tour it might have been shared by the young scallywag who asked Willie John McBride if he had ever played rugby with Robert Muldoon – the New Zealand Prime Minister – and by Roy Laidlaw. The labours of Hercules were slight by comparison with the hardships Laidlaw suffered behind the Lions forwards. Gradually, he had the stuffing knocked out of him. His courage never deserted him but his confidence did and, by the end of the tour, he was playing from memory. Late in the tour there was a brief respite from the buffeting – at Hamilton when, with the Lions forwards dominant, Laidlaw – as one observer aptly put it – 'rode in an armchair', and Waikato, supposedly one of the strongest provincial teams, was routed. Later that week it was no thanks to his forwards that Laidlaw didn't leave Eden Park in a wheelchair following the massacre in the Fourth Test. Laidlaw completed his tour having played in thirteen of the eighteen games including all four Tests. He was as game and uncomplaining at the end as he had been at the beginning. Physically he was in good shape but some psychological damage was surely inevitable.

There was much to chew on in the weeks between the end of the tour and the beginning of the new season. For every excuse there was a scapegoat and for every scapegoat an excuse. The selectors, the selectors of the selectors, the coaching structure, the injuries, the itinerary and the leadership were individually and collectively blamed for the results. Telfer returned home and immediately went to ground. His wife Frances had kept the press cuttings of the tour and, for the next few days, Telfer punished himself mercilessly by reading every word. He was shocked by the savagery of some criticism. He was hurt, dismayed and disillusioned and questioned the wisdom of resuming his duties as Scotland's coach for the forthcoming season. The job had been offered to

Scotland's team at Cardiff. Roy Laidlaw finds something to admire about his skipper

him before he left for New Zealand and he had accepted it; now he was having second thoughts.

In the weeks before the start of the next season, Telfer thought long and hard about the tour. The lowest point undoubtedly had been the 38–6 thrashing at Eden Park. Not only had the Lions failed to win the match, they had failed to win anything. Yes, they had won some provincial matches and many more friends than their predecessors in 1977 – but not the victories by which the tour, the players and the management would be judged. Throughout the tour Telfer had made the point that, until there was uniformity in coaching technique in the four home countries, the Lions would continue to have problems winning test matches unless, of course, there happened to be an unusually large crop of top-class players available to the selectors. In

1983, unfortunately, the planetary system was devoid of stars. Telfer recognized this fact from the outset and regretted that there had been no opportunity to hold squad sessions in the UK prior to departure; but he had still believed that there was enough good basic material to beat the All Blacks. Now, having given the matter careful thought, he was an advocate of the two-coach system – one for the forwards and one for the backs – with one being in overall charge. Telfer knew what he wanted from the backs but did not always know how to transmit his ideas to them. Much of his day was devoted to the forwards and this was time wasted for the backs, among whom no individual emerged as a natural leader. Ollie Campbell, delightful soul though he is, tended to be introspective; only John Carleton appeared to have both the knowledge and the ability to impart it but, as a winger, he was too remote from the play to influence it. The classic example of poor organization among the backs came on the eve of the Third Test at Dunedin when, in freezing conditions and on a waterlogged training ground, they spent the entire session attempting to handle the ball. As preparation for the following day when the conditions were bound to be similar, it was a pointless exercise.

Pondering these things, Telfer was less than ever convinced that he should take on another term as Scotland's coach. But the promise had been made and he could not go back on it. Furthermore, he had been encouraged by the attitude of the Scots in the party. On the flight home from Auckland they had discussed the tour amongst themselves and had repeated their belief that Scotland would have a good season. John Rutherford, for one, was convinced that a Triple Crown was not beyond them and Telfer, although he foresaw problems in the front five of the pack and in the line-out, was not at this stage inclined to dampen the players' enthusiasm.

But the news, in early September, that the All Blacks would be coming to Scotland later that year was not the most welcome piece he received after his decision to stay on.

2   *The All Blacks Return*

The speed and zeal with which New Zealand had supported Her Majesty's Government over the Falklands crisis clearly jeopardized the All Blacks tour to Argentina, scheduled for October and November 1983. Uppermost in the minds of the NZRFU was the security risk involving not only the players but also the supporters and although the tour was still officially on when the Lions left New Zealand in July, contingency plans were already far advanced for an alternative tour. When it became clear that the Argentine tour was a non-starter, the NZRFU gratefully accepted the invitation to tour England and Scotland. The All Blacks would play eight matches, including two internationals on successive Saturdays.

It would not have required an especially astute intellect to deduce from the itinerary that only a side of exceptional quality could come through unbeaten. And this was assuredly not one of the strongest All Blacks sides. How could it be, without the five tight forwards who had been the bedrock of the All Blacks' success against the Lions? Without Knight, Ashworth, Haden. Whetton and their captain Andy Dalton in the forwards, and deprived of the coruscating brilliance of Dave Loveridge at scrum-half, the All Blacks were reduced to the ordinary. They were, in Jim Telfer's words, no better than provincial standard and no one knew better than Telfer what that meant. If the All Blacks lost, even more calumny would be heaped on the Lions. On the other hand, if Scotland won, much of the gloss would be removed by the knowledge that they had done so against inferior opposition.

Nevertheless, the All Blacks were not completely shorn of class. They came with the back row that had dismantled the Lions in the Test series: Jock Hobbs, Mark Shaw, the most durable and destructive of the New Zealand flankers, and Murray Mexted, generally acknowledged to be the finest number 8 in the world. Behind, the tourists could field five of their Test back division, including the magical Maori, Steve Pokere and Stu Wilson who, somewhat controversially, had been given the captaincy in Dalton's absence. Many believed that the captaincy should have been offered to Mexted; when it was later discovered that the number 8 had not even been entrusted with the leadership of the pack, rumours spread of a personality clash between Mexted and the All Blacks' coach, Bryce Rope – rumours which, for the duration of the tour at any rate, were utterly without foundation. If Mexted was never quite at his best, he was nevertheless a tower of strength in this makeshift New Zealand pack.

However much the Lions may have gibbed at their itinerary in New Zealand, it paled into insignificance beside the fiendish schedule presented to the All Blacks. What devious mind, they must have asked themselves, could have conjured up a game under lights at Leicester against possibly the strongest of the English divisions, four days before the international against Scotland? Typically, the All Blacks swallowed their medicine without a murmur of protest. They even claimed that they preferred it this way. What was good enough for Andy Leslie's All Blacks – when

This will hurt you a lot more than me, boyo. Steve Munro takes Dacey's tackle at Cardiff

they had played undefeated against Ireland, a Welsh XV and the Barbarians in the space of a week, was certainly good enough for Wilson's side.

For the opening game against Edinburgh, there were nine new All Blacks in the side. Edinburgh selected four full internationalists, three of whom were in the scrum where it was felt that they might severely embarrass the tourists. The All Blacks' scrummage had been causing them problems in practice and at one stage Scott Crichton and Kevin Boroevich, the two props selected for the first game at Myreside, had looked anything but comfortable against an opposition pack brought up to full strength by two members of the Edinburgh under-21 side. In the event, the tourists were carried through by some of the traditional All Black virtues – the low driving of their forwards and their speed to the loose ball – and beat Edinburgh comfortably, if not entirely convincingly, by 22–6. The most worrying aspect for the tourists was the number of penalties they conceded. Of the forty awarded by the referee Lawrie Prideaux during the match, twenty-four went against them. Their sole consolation on the day was that Peter Steven, the Edinburgh kicker, was so dismally off form that he missed six out of seven attempts at goal, four of them in the first quarter when Edinburgh were seeking to establish an early lead with the wind at their backs. Steven did kick one penalty and Gavin Hastings another, but it was scant reward for Edinburgh's lively and, at times, adventurous start.

Frank Shelford scored the All Blacks' first try of the tour after Pokere had effortlessly outflanked the Edinburgh defence. Wilson and Craig Green scored the tourists' other tries; Robbie Deans chipped in with two penalties and two conversions. The All Blacks were happy enough with the win but not with the high proportion of penalties given against them. The spherical Crichton on the tight head had been penalized on several occasions for collapsing the scrum. Bryce

Rope argued that, far from wilfully lowering the scrums, Crichton had been exhausting himself trying to keep Alex Brewster, his opposite number, upright. Edinburgh retorted that as they had been in command of the scrummage throughout the game, they would have had no wish to 'kill the goose'. . . . Fairest, perhaps, to conclude that neither side scrummaged particularly well.

But the South of Scotland, who were next on the All Blacks agenda and who had dispatched spies to Myreside, were guardedly optimistic about their chances of becoming the first side in history to defeat the All Blacks in Scotland. Their optimism was misplaced. Once every so often a

'Behind you Roy' – David Leslie racing to Laidlaw's assistance against Wales

team so excels itself that it sets new standards in one or more phases of play. The 1971 Lions had attained the seemingly unattainable in the fifth game of their tour against Wellington; the Barbarians had reached sublime heights against Ian Kirkpatrick's All Blacks; the North of England had given as near a flawless display, against Graham Mourie's tourists, as had been achieved by any British provincial side; and on Saturday, 29 October 1983 at Netherdale, Stu Wilson's All Blacks were quite irresistible. The level of performance is of course related to the quality of the opposition – and it must be said that on the day the South of Scotland could hardly be classed as worthy opponents. They disintegrated in the face of the All Blacks' closely supported forward assaults in which Hika Reid, Hobbs, Shaw and the magnificent Mexted were free to do much as they pleased. Pokere glided through the proceedings – a class apart. It was of no significance whatsoever that the South were only two points behind at halftime and that, theoretically, they were still in the hunt with eight minutes of the game remaining. They were outclassed and the final result of 30–6 to the tourists hardly reflected the gulf between the two sides.

In the South's defence, they were dealt a serious blow on the eve of the match when their

Cuthbertson and Tomes on hand to support Paxton

captain Jim Aitken withdrew because of a flu virus. They might have held onto the towel for a while longer had Aitken been there to chivvy them along. The South were also greatly handicapped by an injury to David Leslie whose departure with a gashed leg left Hobbs as the sole guardian of the loose ball. Nevertheless, the South was the flagship of Scottish district rugby in 1983 and with eleven internationalists, seven of whom were about to be selected for Scotland, they should not have capitulated as they did. The area of greatest concern for the Scotland selectors was in the second row, where the South experiment of playing two locks with the bulk and ballast of Tom Smith and Alan Tomes had not been a success. With a front row of Aitken, Deans and Milne, the Scots could be sure of a solid base from their scrummage, but the line-out was a different matter. The All Blacks, even with locks as raw as Albert Anderson and Gary Braid, had won in their own inimitable style the major share of line-out ball against the South. Without Leslie and Iain Paxton who, like Leslie, had to be replaced in the second half, the South had been at the mercy of Mexted at the tail of the line-out.

It was crucial that the Scots got their line-out balance right, blending height, weight, mobility and, not least, guile. The height and bulk were provided by Tom Smith, who was awarded his second cap, having won his first against England the previous season. The guile was provided by Bill Cuthbertson, who had impressed the New Zealanders with his knowledge of the game during Scotland's tour in 1981 and who was no stranger to the unorthodox line-out methods of the Antipodean forwards. Furthermore, he was playing well for his new club, Harlequins. With David Leslie unfit, the selectors picked John Beattie, primarily a number 8, on the flank. On their tour to South Africa in 1980, the Lions had tried unsuccessfully to convert Beattie to the side

Elementary my dear Moriarty. Leslie shows the Welshman the way at a lineout

It's never too late. Jim Aitken, the senior citizen in the championship, scores his first international try in the closing stages of the Welsh game

of the scrum, but he had been playing there for Glasgow impressively enough to convince the selectors that he was the right man for the job. As he had shown against Joinel in Paris the previous season, he could be a most aggressive and abrasive opponent and his inclusion would give Scotland the luxury of a fourth jumper.

There was a new cap in the Scotland side – the six-foot-five Watsonian centre, Euan Kennedy. Kennedy, like Beattie, had not been an original selection. David Johnston and Keith Robertson had been paired together in the centre but when Robertson subsequently sprang a collarbone Kennedy was called in, belatedly at the age of 29, for his first cap. A week before the international, Peter Dods played for Gala in a league game against Kelso at Poynder Park and, having missed three out of four kicks at goal, he made way for Dave Bryson.

But on the Tuesday before the game there was better news for Scotland when the Midlands beat the tourists 19–13 at Leicester. Despite the fact that it took two gargantuan kicks by Dusty Hare to secure the win, this was proof positive that the All Blacks were more vulnerable than they had been at any time since 1977. The Midlands had been masters in the line-out, solid in the scrum and most surprising of all given the calibre of the opposition, had been superior in the loose. The formula was simple with the Leicester half backs, Youngs and Cusworth, playing what is popularly known nowadays as 'percentage rugby'. It was the blueprint which England used ten days later to beat the All Blacks although the Midlands frequently made use of their outside backs, a risk never taken by England.

The following day the All Blacks announced their side. There were six new caps but wherever possible the tourists had opted for experience. Of the five tight forwards only Hika Reid had played in an international. Scott Crichton and Brian McGrattan, both from Wellington, were the props. Albert Anderson and Gary Braid locked the scrum and the two uncapped backs were Andrew Donald at scrum-half and the Canterbury full back Robbie Deans. There had been a rumour that Bernie Fraser might be replaced on the left wing. It had been clear for some time that he was running on reduced power, that his fits of pique were occurring with greater frequency and that he was no longer trustworthy in defence. Bruce Smith, the reserve wing on the tour, had shown up well and on current form was much the sharper of the two. But here again the selectors went for experience and Fraser was awarded his twenty-first cap. He, along with Wilson and Mexted, were the three survivors of the side who had beaten Scotland at Murrayfield in 1979. The three-quarter line was, therefore, the one which had played in all four Tests against the Lions. At stand-off Wayne Smith reclaimed the place he lost because of injury to Ian Dunn in the Final Test. He had played with immense authority during the tour and even in adversity against the Midlands had produced many delightful touches.

For the Scots there were some heartening signs at the All Blacks training session at Riccarton on the Thursday. To begin with, it was not a good session. A greasy ball and greatly reduced visibility did not help, but there was also a freneticism not normally associated with All Blacks' preparations. With so many newcomers in the party, Bryce Rope had consistently emphasized the need for steady rather than spectacular progress. But some of the more experienced players were becoming impatient to explore the frontiers which, after the annihilation of the South, seemed well within their compass. Since the midweek defeat at Leicester, Rope had been at pains to remind his players of the need for simplicity and to extol the traditional strength of New Zealand rugby. On the evidence of that

Thursday's training session, there was still some gentle persuasion to be done. Wilson promised a shorter, sharper session the next day. He had not been misled by the All Blacks' brilliance at Netherdale; he recognized it for what it was – not so much a triumphant procession for the tourists as an abandonment of hope by the South. If that impoverished display was the best that Scotland had to offer then there could be only one result in the international. On the other hand, the doggedness of the Scottish character was surely embodied in Jim Telfer who had, after all, answered his own question – 'Is there life after a losing Lions tour?' – by his refusal to go into a self-imposed exile and by his acceptance of another term as national coach.

For Telfer there was one major difference between working with Scotland and with the Lions. The Scots understood his thinking and would more readily accede to his demands. Most of them had toured with him in New Zealand and Australia, they had watched his plans evolve over a number of years, they admired him and above all they respected his judgement. Telfer also knew that in Scotland's colours his players would not leap for the lifeboats as the South had done. He had no qualms about the scrummage. He had first-class half backs and a back row which, on its day, would be the equal of those black-hooded demons Hobbs, Shaw and Mexted. Telfer's main worry was the line-out. The All Blacks were happy enough with parity at the scrummage but it was from the line-outs that they would feed their ravenous backs. Whereas the Lions had been faced with a triumvirate of Haden, Whetton and Mexted, only the latter had returned to plague the Scots. Nevertheless, Anderson had very quickly got the measure of Tom Smith at Netherdale. On the other hand, Smith would receive better support from Cuthbertson – whose understanding of the Machiavellian aspects of the line-outs was matched only by the New Zealanders themselves – and from Beattie.

On Friday night the Scots discussed these and

many other things: their support of the man with the ball, the need for good quality rucking and their tackling. They also prayed that Dods would kick his goals. There are many full backs technically more proficient than Peter Dods. There are certainly those who are fleeter of foot and can make more timely intrusions into a three-quarter line. But few possess a sounder temperament.

On his run up to the conversion of Jim Pollock's last-minute try which, had it been successful, would surely have guaranteed his immortality, Dods had not the faintest idea of the score. The kick was out on the east touchline. It was sweetly hit and sailed majestically towards the posts but shaved the right hand upright. Stu Wilson estimated that it had missed by the width of a post and that is much as it appeared to Dods from where he stood. Only then did he permit himself a look at the scoreboard – 25–25. It was not a disaster but an heroic failure because Dods, as much as anyone that day, had kept the Scots in the game.

A share of 50 points had not been unanimously forecast as the result. It was, by 10 points, Scotland's highest score against the All Blacks and although they were outscored in tries by three to one and had disappointed some by the rigidness of their approach, their tactical plan was undoubtedly the right one on the day. Aitken's leadership was once again of such quality that it caused one to wonder how much more effective would the South have been under his command. Tom Smith's game was a revelation and, on several surging drives upfield, an inspiration. He set up one ruck which must have been the envy of the All Blacks themselves. It was the finest display of rucking produced by the Scots all season. Smith received valiant support from Cuthbertson whose speed around the field was one of the principal reasons for the Scots rucking so much better than the Lions had done. The back row, apart from a tendency to fall offside, which on this occasion went unpunished, demanded admira-

tion for their spirit and close support. All three put in withering tackles; as a consequence the All Blacks were forced to do most of their attacking from the middle distance. This they did twice, however, with deadly effect. Fraser scored on both occasions. Andrew Donald initiated the first after Mexted had appeared to pass out of the tackle. Left with only Dods to beat, Fraser chipped ahead and won the race to the touchdown. He did the same again in the second half when Jock Hobbs exploded from a thicket of forwards in support of Donald.

The first All Black try was typically opportunist. It was scored by Hobbs after Baird had been a little too easily dispossessed by Wilson in touch and Mexted had taken a quick throw. It gave the All Blacks the lead for the first time in the game, John Rutherford having earlier dropped two goals, with his second equalling Ian McGeechan's Scottish record of seven. Deans had kicked a penalty for obstruction on Fraser and his conversion of Fraser's first try gave the tourists a 13–6 lead which by halftime, by dint of Dods' accuracy, Scotland had reduced to a more manageable deficit of 16–15.

The Scottish pack had received splendid support from their half backs and from the strapping Kennedy, whose ability to remain on his feet while protecting the ball was a rare bonus for his forwards. The tourists confessed afterwards that they had not expected Rutherford to play the way he did. They thought that he would run at them and expressed some disappointment that he had played so cagily. But Rutherford gave a masterly demonstration of precise kicking, sending the ball to all corners of the field and forcing the All Blacks from their well-grooved paths. Of the many instances of Scottish bravery in defence, none had a more profound effect than his crushing tackle on Donald. Roy Laidlaw, latterly so tired and harassed with the Lions in New Zealand, played as if relieved of a terrible burden.

The second half was one of almost unparalleled excitement and incident. Fraser scored his second

Would you believe it! Leslie, Calder and Rutherford offer their congratulations

try. Deans converted. Dods kicked his fourth penalty from four attempts, then his fifth. Deans replied with his third penalty and the All Blacks led 25–21. The denouement was as swift as it was unexpected. The Scots rather fortuitously gained possession from a line-out near the All Blacks' line. The ball flew down the three-quarters from Rutherford to Johnston who held back until he saw the whites of Pokere's eyes before kicking diagonally through for Pollock. With the advantage of Murrayfield's generous in-goal area and a fraction of a second's start over Fraser and Robbie Deans, Pollock was first to the ball and the scores were level. The final act of kicking the winning conversion, albeit from the touchline, must by now have seemed laughably simple to a crowd intoxicated by what was going on.

Dods' kick was not, however, the finale but merely the prelude to a controversy which continued until the end of the tour and in which the principals were the opposing wings, Pollock and Fraser, and the Scottish touch judge, Brian Anderson. Pollock, it appears, tackled Fraser into touch without the ball. Fraser, whose tolerance threshold is lower than most, aimed a swipe at Pollock and Anderson raised his flag. Meanwhile play was progressing at a furious pace towards the Scottish line. With the scores level, the French referee, René Hourquet, penalized the Scots for offside. At this point the referee's attention was drawn to the touch judge's raised flag and, following his discussion with Brian Anderson,

Hourquet reversed his decision. Instead of the All Blacks kicking for goal, the Scots kicked to touch and the final whistle sounded.

The All Blacks were incensed. They claimed that Fraser had been taken out of the game illegally and that Anderson's intervention had denied them the chance of winning the game. They complained of too much interference from the touchlines and later that night, before they had given themselves the benefit of calm reflection, they requested that Brian Anderson, who was scheduled to run the line at Twickenham the following week, be replaced. Their request was turned down but it was an unfortunate end to a magnificent game.

Of all the comments made afterwards, two put the events into perspective. One came from Aitken, who said, 'We have taken a couple of steps forward. There is a long way to go – but it's a start.' The second observation came from Paul Mitchell, the All Blacks' manager. 'It's marvellous,' he said, 'to see Jim Telfer smile.' To which all who had followed the Lions' convulsive progress through New Zealand and who had shared in Telfer's disappointments, simply added, 'Hear, hear.'

3 Trials and Tribulations

An hour before they kicked off against New Zealand, the Scots had learned of Wales' 24–6 defeat by Rumania in Bucharest. The result was of significance both in the long and short terms because at the end of the season Scotland were due to tour Rumania and, more immediately, they would open their championship campaign against Wales at Cardiff. It was Wales' biggest overseas defeat since 1969 and one which emphasized Rumania's claims to be recognized as a major force in European rugby. But Scotland's first assignment was to beat Wales in January.

In the aftermath of the All Blacks game, John Rutherford discovered that he had played out the last thirty minutes with a broken jaw and Jim Aitken had torn a leg muscle. England meanwhile picked two new caps to play New Zealand, Colin White at loose head prop and Paul Simpson on the flank, for their game against New Zealand, and the Scottish selectors announced their B side to play Ireland at Melrose. Douglas Wyllie, the gifted young Stewarts Melville stand-off who had been called up as a replacement for the All Blacks game when Colin Gass withdrew with injury, partnered Gordon Hunter at half back, and David Sole, the 22-year-old Exeter student, was surprisingly preferred to Highland's Gregor Mackenzie at loose head. Sole was one of five Anglo-Scots in a side which was useful, but which contained a hard core of experience in the pack.

England, with an all-consuming display of forward power, pulverized the All Blacks at Twickenham and by so doing sowed the seeds of their own destruction later in the season. Unlike Telfer, England's new coach, Dick Greenwood, failed to make an accurate evaluation of the All Blacks' standing in relation to other international sides.

In addition to New Zealand's tour to Scotland and England, and the Welsh visit to Rumania, Australia had toured France, Japan had been to Wales and Canada had played against an England XV at Twickenham. Ireland alone of the countries competing in the international championship had not had the benefit of a warm-up match. The B international against Scotland was, therefore, of considerable importance to them. The selectors had drawn heavily on the Leinster side which had won the provincial title for the fourth time in five years. In the pack were Mick Moylett, seen as the natural successor to Moss Keane at lock, and Derek McGrath, described as the young Fergus Slattery. In the centre was another promising youngster, Brendan Mullin, who had been saddled with the onerous burden of being likened to Mike Gibson. In the event neither Mullin nor McGrath were given the chance to look even remotely like themselves, much less like Gibson or Slattery.

By beating Ireland 22–13 the Scots gained their most emphatic win in the series against the Irish and the selectors gained confirmation of the fact that there was a first-class half-back pairing in reserve to Rutherford and Laidlaw, a full back of great promise in Gavin Hastings, a lock of international class in Alister Campbell and two fine loose forwards in John Jeffrey and Finlay Calder. Had it not been for the fact that the Scots

Hello, hello, hello – one of the few loose balls to escape the Scottish back row at Cardiff and Butler seems surprised

missed seven kicks at goal, the Irish would have been swept overboard.

A truer reflection of the difference between the sides was to be found in the try count, which finished at four to one in Scotland's favour. The Scots teamwork produced two tries in the first ten minutes, the first by Wyllie who, as he grew in confidence, began to resurrect many of the old and almost forgotten skills of his position. He made better use of the blind side than any other Scottish stand-off since Colin Telfer. Iwan Tukalo scored Scotland's second with a searing burst down the left wing in pursuit of Hunter's kick ahead. Later in the game Hunter dropped a goal, Peter Steven kicked an incredible penalty from his own half and scored a try, and Tukalo scored his second with another fine run and deftly placed kick ahead.

The interdistrict championship, the precursor to the trial, confirmed only that it is an anachronism in its present form, an intrusion into the league season. The South, who had been so savagely mauled by the All Blacks, won the title at a canter and the only minor surprise was Glasgow's victory over Edinburgh in the Intercity match at Hughenden where John Beattie excelled.

National trials are perhaps the only occasions when the selectors are blameless. They do, after all, choose both sides. The selectors very properly kept faith with the majority of those who had played against the All Blacks, the two notable exceptions being Roy Laidlaw at scrum-half and the number 8 Iain Paxton, who were selected for the Whites. Euan Kennedy, a flu victim, withdrew belatedly from the side and was replaced in the centre by Jim Renwick.

The selectors introduced into the Whites XV a

Rutherford at last gets into his stride against Wales

number of players in key positions who could be relied upon to enliven the proceedings. In order to ensure that the occasion didn't fall flat, they gave David Leslie the captaincy of the junior side. Leslie had by now fully recovered from the gashed leg which had denied him his cap against the All Blacks, but he had played in only one game since his injury and had doubted that he would be picked for the trial. He would not be drawn on the subject but those closest to him knew how deeply hurt he had been by his omission from the Lions tour. Of the many bizarre decisions made by that selection committee none was more preposterous than the rejection of Leslie. Not only was he omitted from the original selection, he was third behind the Englishmen Nick Jeavons and David Cooke in the list of replacements. He was, therefore, ranked outside the top ten back row forwards in Britain yet, on his performance in

Paris alone, he should have been an automatic choice.

Despite his 24 caps and the fact that he was generally considered to be one of the finest flank forwards in the country, Leslie nevertheless felt that he still had something to prove and this was as good an opportunity as any for him. He had many things in his favour. There were at least seven Whites who could reasonably expect promotion. In the pack, Leslie himself and Iain Paxton had the smell of international competition in their nostrils. So did Tomes and Campbell. Roy Laidlaw, having been supplanted in the South side by Gordon Hunter, would not surrender his Scotland place without a fight and in the three-quarter line were Keith Robertson and Steve Munro, fit again and anxious to reclaim their places. The Whites, in short, were the natural party of opposition. Although the margin

Scotland v. England. Was that a sidestep by Alan Tomes or did Bainbridge trip? Either way Nick Youngs grits his

teeth and moves in for the tackle. Les Cusworth just grits his teeth

Here come the cavalry – Leslie supports Rutherford's charge against Wales

of their eventual victory over the Blues by 21 points to 3 was rather larger than the selectors would have wished, the game was neither the embarrassment nor the farce it was made out to be in some quarters.

It had been clear from the outset that the Blues would have to reproduce their finest form to survive. They failed, and it was better that they did so in a trial at Murrayfield than against Wales at the National Stadium. The organization, motivation and appetite of the oppositon were im-

mediately apparent. Leslie's display demanded that he be picked for Cardiff, as did Paxton's. Laidlaw, admittedly behind an advancing platform, had much the better of his duel with Hunter. Tomes had a good game against Tom Smith whose activities had been curtailed by a serious knee injury the previous month. Munro and Robertson also merited inclusion. Strictly on the evidence of the trial, the Scottish XV for Cardiff should contain four of the Whites forwards and three or even four of the backs.

4 Cardiff Reconquered

When the selectors announced their side for Cardiff it was a predictable amalgam of the Blues and the Whites. The result was an eminently sensible and well-balanced XV being, in all but three positions, the one which had drawn with the All Blacks. Where they might have been tempted to gamble on Alister Campbell's mobility or to broaden their horizons behind the scrum by picking Gordon Hunter at scrum-half, they kept faith with those who had served them well in the past and those who would not be unnerved by the Cardiff experience. There were no new caps and all but Steve Munro, Peter Dods and Euan Kennedy had previously sampled Cardiff's unique atmosphere.

The overwhelming superiority of the Whites in the trial was reflected in the fact that five members of that side had been promoted. Leslie and Paxton returned and so did Roy Laidlaw. His resilience and fortitude were to be priceless assets in the forthcoming campaign, although one felt sorry for Hunter who had patiently served his apprenticeship in the national squad since 1981 and had completed his baker's dozen as a replacement. In the almost certain knowledge that the Welsh would pick the volcanic John Perkins as their front jumper, the Scots opted for Bill Cuthbertson and recalled Alan Tomes who had played well in the trial. Tom Smith's international career had been blighted by injury once again. Steve Munro, the Ayr wing and another bedevilled by injury, replaced Jim Pollock, the idea being that he would add support to Kennedy's midfield bursts from the right flank.

Scotland's tactical plan was clear from the composition of the side and would vary in few respects from the type of game they had played against the All Blacks. It made sense because there were similarities between the All Blacks and Wales who possessed fast, clever backs but who, on the evidence of the Rumanian game, lacked the necessary power up front. When the Welsh side was announced, it found little public support in the Principality. Eleven of the side so badly beaten in Rumania were retained and Mark Douglas, the Llanelli scrum-half, was the sole member of the Welsh B side which had beaten France, to be promoted to the national XV.

In defence of the selectors it should be said that their choice was severely restricted by the retirement of Jeff Squires and Graham Price and by the injury to Terry Holmes. But they had surprised many by preferring Staff Jones at loose head prop to Ian Stephens whose Lions tour, though brought to a premature end because of injury, should have proved conclusively that he was the best loose head in the four home countries. Ian Eidman on the tight head was probably good enough to have kept Price out of the side. Holmes and Squire, however, were irreplaceable. In the previous season they had covered up so many of the Welsh deficiencies and now in their absence there were no ready-made replacements. Ray Giles had been the scrum-half in Bucharest and had not provided the answer to the problem. The selectors seemed reluctant to risk the wayward talent of Pontypool's David Bishop and so decided to introduce Douglas who in style was not dissimilar to Holmes.

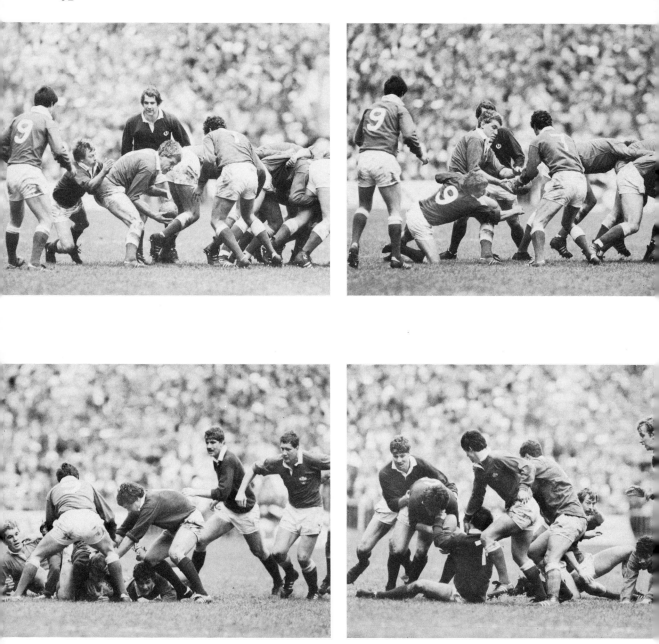

Now see here little fellow – this is man's business. Laidlaw getting in amongst the Welsh forwards and showing

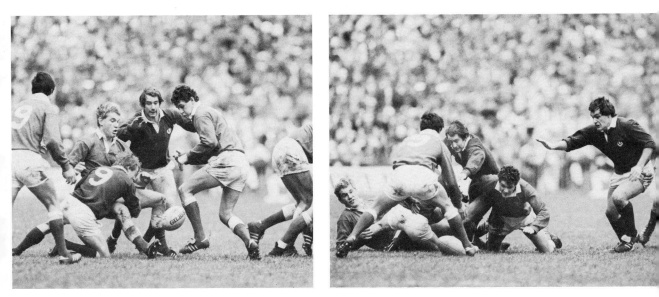

that persistence brings its rewards

Paxton finishes

It was the back row selection, however, which aroused the most heated debate in Wales. Fearing a repeat of the Rumanian disaster when the Welsh had gone into the match without a genuine middle jumper in their line-out and had been completely overwhelmed at the back by the telescopic number 8 Stefan Constantin, the selectors quite rightly recalled Bob Norster, who had recovered from injury. He was unarguably one of the two best line-out men in the country. But to the bafflement of almost an entire nation they picked Richard Moriarty as a blind-side flanker. In his six previous appearances for Wales, Moriarty had played as a lock although he had played much of his club rugby with Swansea at number 8. To select him out of position against a back row and half backs as experienced as Scotland's seemed an extraordinary gamble. 'It is not a gamble,' said one of the selectors memorably, 'but a calculated risk.' The statement seemed as illogical as the selec-

tion. Moriarty was clearly in the side first and foremost for his value as a line-out player but he had neither the reflexes nor the mobility to compete with the athletic Scots in the air or on the ground. As it happened this was less of a problem than Moriarty's failure to subdue Leslie at the line-out, nevertheless it was undoubtedly the season's worst piece of miscasting.

Apart from the grave doubts surrounding Moriarty there was concern in Wales that the side was critically short of experience. Only two players, Butler with eleven caps and Ackerman with twelve, had reached double figures. Their caps totalled sixty-two against the two hundred and sixty-six on the Scottish side. The gulf in experience became even more pronounced when firstly, Mark Wyatt, who had made such a fine impression the previous season, broke a bone in his hand and was replaced by the uncapped Bridgend full back Howell Davies, and secondly, on the eve of the match, when Ian Eidman withdrew suffering from a virus infection. His place at tight head prop was taken by Rhys Morgan of Newport and, like Davies, a new cap.

Adhering to their plan of two years previously, when they had trounced Wales at Cardiff, the Scots travelled south to Chepstow on the Thursday night and ran out at the Army Apprentices College on the Friday morning. The build-up was relaxed, the weather bright and mild and the mood one of quiet confidence. The squad, with very few changes, had been through a lot together: tours to France, New Zealand and Australia, a victory at Twickenham in the final match of the previous season and a draw with the All Blacks. They knew that they had a massive advantage in key areas. Rutherford and Laidlaw were playing together for the nineteenth time in a major international. Wales, on the other hand, was fielding the eighth half-back combination in sixteen matches. Jim Telfer's attempts to attach some credence to the selection of Moriarty, by asserting that he should be able to adapt quickly to

Gotcha! Paxton, Milne and Tomes steal round on Douglas . . . But to no avail

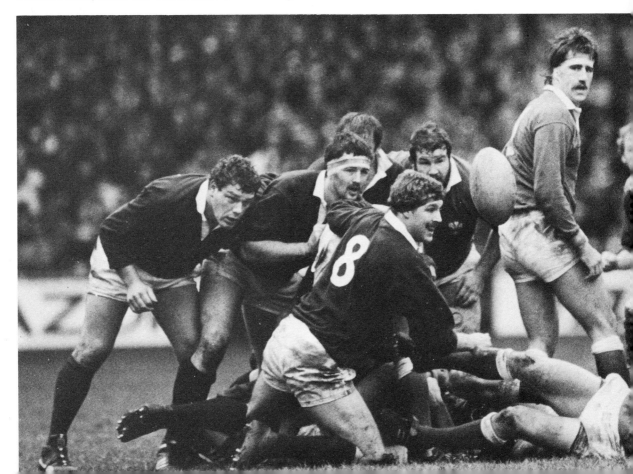

his new surroundings, could not conceal the fact that the Scots were massively confident of winning the battle in the loose. As a result they felt that they would win the war.

If the result was predictable the manner of it was not. The Scots won 15–9, but had chances enough to double the score. But there were times throughout the game when the match could just as easily have swung Wales' way and in the final ten minutes the Scots were fighting a desperate rearguard action to protect their lead. It was a fierce contest, frequently abrasive and punctuated by outbursts of ill-temper with Wales committing more acts of crass stupidity in one game than most sides manage in an entire season. The Scots in the main held themselves in check while Jim Aitken, under whose captaincy they had yet to lose, added to his stature both as the skipper and as a player by scoring the decisive try – his first in international rugby. His forwards responded magnificently, their solidity in the tight and instinctive awareness in the loose overcoming several defensive lapses and a disjointed back division.

In simple terms, the Scots channelled their energies more effectively than Wales and, as everyone had predicted, the choice of Moriarty was fatal. With Moriarty detailed to look after Leslie at the tail, David Pickering, the fastest of the Welsh back row, was caught up in the midst of the line-out maelstrom and was of little assistance to his beleaguered colleagues in the loose. These frustrations no doubt contributed to Welsh intemperance, but their attitude was duly punished by the Irish referee Owen Doyle. The fact that this was his first international match may have explained his reluctance to send Moriarty off the field. He warned the Welshman on two occasions: once for an unprovoked assault on Calder at the line-out and again for stamping in a ruck. By their indiscipline the Welsh forwards undid much of the splendid work of the backs, among whom Dacey at stand-off and the two young three-quarters Bowen and Titley confirmed the promise they had displayed in earlier

matches. Dacey, in particular, played a mature game and on the day outshone his more illustrious opponent John Rutherford, who was unusually prodigal with the possession he received in the first half and was hesitant on a number of occasions.

Roy Laidlaw, however, displayed all his old perkiness, once breaking through the Welsh defence and sending Paxton clear. Had Paxton clung onto the ball he would surely have scored, but the number 8 had done well to support Laidlaw's burst and earlier had scored the Scots' opening try. The legitimacy of this score might have been questioned, with at least one forward pass in the movement, but it was cleverly conceived. From a free kick, the Scots swung towards the right touchline, Rutherford flipped the ball to Leslie whose scoring pass to Paxton could most generously be described as straight but which was, in the eyes of at least one observer, 'more like the baton change in a relay race'. It was, nevertheless, a most timely score, coming just before halftime.

Throughout the game all the critical passages of play favoured Scotland. Their defence was coordinated when it mattered most, namely at the beginning of each half and throughout the most determined Welsh rally in the closing minutes. Aitken's try was equally well timed. Wales, 6–3 down at halftime, had regained the lead they had held early in the game when Howell Davies had opened the scoring with a penalty.

In the second half, Mark Douglas breached the Scottish defence as he had done on a number of occasions, putting Titley over in the corner. Leslie then won a line-out on the right and Rutherford, more composed this half than he had been in the first, kicked through for Roger Baird to force a line-out close to the Welsh line. The situation was not dissimilar to the one from which the Scots had scored their match-saving try against the All Blacks. The Scots won possession from the line-out, Milne drove round on an unscheduled peel supported by Laidlaw and

Scotland's defence at Cardiff was sure at the crucial times throughout the game – Mark
Douglas and Bob Ackerman are the Welshmen firmly held in Scotland's grip

Eyes front – Tomes, Cuthbertson and Paxton concentrate on the ball. Colclough has spotted a friend in the stand

Oh no you don't! Nick Youngs cannot break loose from the Scottish defence

Jim Calder is caught by the French but is surrounded by eager helpers

Over to you, Mr Calder. Paxton's progress is halted by Gallion but the Scottish attack continues

Hold on a minute, Davey! The expression on Jim Aitken's face suggests that he must be running. Leslie marks time

Aitken, was shunted from behind by Leslie and barged over.

It was the Scots' third win in five matches against Wales and their second in a row at Cardiff (where previously they had won only three times in 57 years). Although the Scots had not played particularly well, and there had been some leakage down the lefthand side of the scrum where Mark Douglas had concentrated most of his attacks, this win away from home gave the Scots a realistic chance of their first Triple Crown since 1938. Next on the list was England – at Murrayfield.

5 The Hundredth Match

England had been inactive since their greatly acclaimed victory over the All Blacks. They had not been involved in the first series of matches in the international championships, which they regarded as a mixed blessing. It was advantageous in that Peter Wheeler, who had broken his hand in the game against the All Blacks, had more time in which to recover and the same went for Maurice Colclough, who had been incapacitated by a back injury. But England's first game for nearly three months would be against a side that had, two weeks previously, beaten Wales at Cardiff.

Wheeler himself was gravely concerned about the interruption to England's training schedules through injury and bad weather. The trial had not been a failure but neither had it been an unqualified success with England beating The Rest 18–15. The opposition had fielded what was virtually the Gloucester pack and a back division of limited ambition. The two squad sessions prior to the Calcutta Cup match had gone badly, the underfoot conditions at Bisham Abbey having aggravated a number of minor but irritating injuries. The session at Stourbridge had been hindered by the absence of Gary Pearce, their tight head prop, and by the late arrival of Colclough who, more than anyone, required a hard workout. Business commitments combined with his injury had deprived Colclough of regular competitive rugby, so on the Saturday before the international he had arranged a game for himself in the Wasps Second XV. It was little wonder that Dick Greenwood, England's articulate coach, who had succeeded Mike Davis at the start of the season, complained of a certain vagueness amongst the forwards during their first training session in Edinburgh.

The original intention had been for England to train at Peebles, but with the ground frostbound the Rugby Football Union accepted Hibernian Football Club's invitation to use the facilities at Easter Road where there was undersoil heating. But the need to preserve the pitch for a Premier League game that weekend denied England the scrummaging practice they badly needed. Pearce and Colclough were passed fit to play and so was Wheeler who had played for Leicester in a cup tie the previous Saturday. The training session was unsatisfactory. Colclough looked ponderous and overweight as did a number of the other English forwards. To add to their problems, the scrummage session, which had been promised the next day, was disrupted. The local forwards summoned to provide the oppositon failed to materialize so the England scrum packed down against the replacements plus Derek Morgan, the Chairman of the selectors, and sundry other alikadoos.

In the Scottish camp all was progressing smoothly save for the almost inevitable withdrawal of the unfortunate Steve Munro who had to pull out of the international side for the second time in the season. This time it was because of an ankle injury. His replacement was not Jim Pollock, whose late try had saved the game against New Zealand, but the Melrose three-quarter Keith Robertson who, in his twenty-three internationals, had played eighteen times on the wing. The Scots knew from England's selection that they would attempt the same tactics with which they had beaten New Zealand. England would rely heavily on an advancing scrummage, with the solidly built Nick Youngs probing round the fringes and linking with his loose forwards Winterbottom and Simpson. But Jim Telfer gave more thought to the line-out than he did to the scrum. Apart from Leslie, the Scots had won practically nothing from their line-out men against Wales; England, with Colclough and Steve Bainbridge, seemed better equipped than the Welsh in this department. Furthermore, John Scott was no novice at the tail. He would not be so easily duped as Moriarty had been. Telfer, therefore, required something extra from Alan Tomes who had the job of marking Bainbridge. But it had not gone unnoticed North of the Border that from two such potentially fruitful sources as Bainbridge and Colclough, England had extracted a relatively meagre amount of possession against the All Blacks.

The key to the Scots' success, however, lay in the scrummaging. If they could hold the England pack they would, at a stroke, obliterate 75 per cent of England's attacking options. Youngs, denied his launching pad, would have to fall back on his pass, which was not his strongest suit, and Winterbottom and Simpson would have nowhere to go. They knew that Les Cusworth at stand-off had been conditioned, not only by the All Blacks game but also by his experiences against the Scots at Twickenham the previous season, to keep his three-quarters away from the opposiiton loose forwards. If it came to a situation where it was Scotland's ruck against England's maul, Telfer was confident that the rucking side would win the day. But there had to be an overall improvement in John Rutherford's play. He had to be more positive, more assertive.

On the Saturday morning Rutherford watched the rain falling and knew exactly the type of game he would play that afternoon. The century of games between the oldest of international adversaries ended for Scotland as it had begun in 1871

– with a win. Their victory by 18–6 was as decisive as any against the Auld Enemy in recent years. Once again, the Scottish forwards were magnificent – a finely blended unit, alert and supportive. The back row – in which, if distinctions should be made amidst such excellence, Calder was tops – once again prospered in conditions made for rucking. But the toast was to the 'front five' who not only held the English scrum but in the latter stages shifted it backwards.

Perhaps England sensed the worst at the very first scrummage of the game when they were checked and their heel was disrupted. Tomes, in his thirty-fifth international, played one of his best games for Scotland and Cuthbertson mined great chunks of possession from the depths of the rucks and the mauls. John Rutherford made a triumphant return to form. He kicked with unerring accuracy, tugging poor Dusty Hare from one side of the field to the other until the full back had no place to hide. Baird and Robertson harassed him unmercifully on the wings and Johnston and Kennedy came at him down the middle. Slemen, a reliable henchman on similar occasions in the past, was this time unable to offer Hare adequate assistance. Barry John had carried out a similar blitz on Fergie McCormack when the 1971 Lions had beaten New Zealand in the First Test at Dunedin and, like McCormack on that occasion, Hare's whole act went to pieces. The most prolific scorer in the history of the game, Hare missed six kicks at goal from eight attempts and Youngs was under too much pressure to match the accuracy of Rutherford's tactical kicking.

The severest criticism of England's play was their blind adherence to a plan which was patently not working. They were playing rugby by numbers with an innumerate side. Fitness was another factor. Wheeler, who had played only three games since November, was out of touch both as a player and as captain. Colclough was a passenger and Simpson, who had so relished his confrontation with the All Blacks, seemed less than interested with the ball behind him. When Winterbottom left

A try in the making – Euan Kennedy's dash for the England line. Could have been closer to the posts, Euan, but well done all the same. Peter Dods offers his congratulations before attempting the conversion

the field in the second half with a hip injury, England lost their most consistently committed forward.

Scotland were much faster in thought and deed. Rutherford's first kick wickedly flighted across field, had it stuck in Johnston's outstretched hands, it would have produced a try. Later in the game, Laidlaw's chip to the line eluded Baird's grasp and another angled kick from the scrum-half put Slemen into a dizzy spin. The first try highlighted the superiority of the Scots' reactions. The ball squirted into midfield from a line-out and with both England centres overrunning it, Paxton hacked on and Johnston dribbled past Hare to score. Thereafter, it became clear that if England couldn't kick their goals they wouldn't score. Once in the first half they had looked like manufacturing a try but fatal indecision in front of the posts had blown their chance. Hare meanwhile was missing kick after kick – four to be exact – while Woodward tried unsuccessfully to drop a goal. Eventually Hare's persistence was rewarded just before halftime with a forty-yard penalty.

Another timely try by Scotland dealt England a grievous blow within a minute of play restarting. Laidlaw's kick down the West touchline once again revealed the Scots' speed over the ground but more significantly exposed Hare's lack of it. Calder won the ball, Tomes drove forward and with England's defence caught flat, Kennedy scored Scotland's second try. Dods, with the accuracy and composure that had followed him throughout his international career to this point, converted and kicked two more penalties before the end whilst Hare kicked one and missed two

others. Throughout the game, however, the greatest danger to Scotland had come not from England but from their own indiscipline which, on three occasions, had lost them ground while they argued with David Burnett, the referee. On the day their imprudence went unpunished but it could just as easily have cost them the game.

The Scots now had their clearest sight of the Triple Crown for forty-six years. The prize had been within their reach several times during these barren years, but never before in Dublin where they had last won the Triple Crown in 1933. There was a confidence about this side and a sense of purpose in all that they did which augured well for the forthcoming trip to Lansdowne Road.

Jim Telfer had been meticulous in his preparations for the games against Wales and England. On the morning of the Calcutta Cup match he had gone down to the ground. When he returned he talked with some of the senior members of the side and the battle plans were laid. Teamwork in fact had been fundamental to the Scots' success. The selectors, under the convenorship of Ian MacGregor, had done their groundwork. They knew their players and, importantly, they listened to their opinions.

For the next international game, the decision was taken to break with the tradition of staying under the same roof as the Irish side in Dublin. Instead the Scots set up their headquarters on the outskirts of the city. It was an excellent decision. The Irish have probably done more softening up with their seductive blarney in the Shelbourne Hotel than they have ever done in the first twenty minutes of battle at Lansdowne Road.

6 The Thistle in the Crown

The perfectly understandable desire of Scotland's rugby connections to keep Triple Crown hysteria to within reasonable proportions was doomed from the start. Television crews were rushing hither and thither – one group even took up residence in Jim Telfer's hotel in Selkirk. Jim Aitken was much in demand to attend sports dinners, rotary lunches and champagne breakfasts. The planes and boats to Dublin had been fully booked since the Calcutta Cup victory. They had been through it all before, of course, several times since 1938, but somehow the optimism did not feel at all misplaced on this occasion. For the first time since the war the Scots would be playing for the Triple Crown in Dublin, not Twickenham where so many disasters had befallen them. It was not that Dublin had been a particularly happy ground for the Scots – they had only won once there since 1966. But this Scotland side had much in its favour, not least its own spirit and confidence built up over three years of playing, training and touring together.

Telfer, so dispirited after the Lions debacle, had, with the help of the players who had accompanied him to New Zealand, turned the lessons of that tour to his advantage. He knew more about the strength and weaknesses of the opposition than any other British coach. He was fortunate too in that the Scottish Lions had retained their form. Seven of the eight who toured were playing in the Scottish side and John Beattie, who was in competition with his fellow Lion Iain Paxton for the number 8 position, was in fine form and was in the squad. Ireland, on the other hand,

were by any standards a poor international side. Their ageing forwards had aged still more in the opening game against France at Parc des Princes – a brutal encounter during which Garuet, the French prop, was sent off for trying to prise John O'Driscoll's eyes from their sockets. The captains, Rives and Fitzgerald, compounded the felony by subjecting Clive Norling, the referee, to the fifth degree throughout the game. It was an exhibition which hardly portrayed rugby as a game for the sons of gentlefolk.

Ireland had dropped Fergus Slattery, who was palpably unfit in Paris, for their next game against Wales but the result had been no more encouraging. For the English game at Twickenham, the selectors dropped both centres David Irwin and Rory Moroney, the scrum-half Robbie McGrath and Jim McCoy, the tight head prop. They also used the head injury sustained in the game against Wales as the excuse for not picking Fitzgerald and replaced the ailing Ollie Campbell with Tony Ward as stand-off.

With the Scots inactive on the day of the Ireland/England game, Jim Telfer had taken himself off to Twickenham. He was not impressed by what he saw. Ireland went down to their third successive defeat and for the third game in a row failed to score a try. England could and should have won by more than 12–9. Despite the lead given to them by Willie Duggan, who had taken over the captaincy from Fitzgerald, the Irish played without conviction. They were vulnerable at full back and open to attack close to the scrum. But there were warning signals for Telfer. Tony

John O'Driscoll meets the immovable hulk in Iain Milne while Calder and Paxton prepare to rescue the ball

Ward, who was playing in his first full international for three years, was understandably fallible in some of his judgements but his goal kicking could not be faulted. He kicked three penalties of varying length but each one a gem of timing and accuracy. The Scots would, therefore, have to guard against the indiscipline which had surfaced during the Calcutta Cup. Donal Lenihan ruled the line-out single-handed and was the more dangerous for being able to play with equal facility at the front or in the middle. This was perhaps just as well for Ireland because, according to some, the only time that Moss Keane had left the ground that season had been on Ireland's flights to Paris and London. And yet Keane had shown at Twickenham that he had at least one more game in him. Indeed one or two of the older spirits were rekindled that day and it was something of a surprise when the Irish announced their side for the Scotland game and included Derek McGrath, a new cap, on the flank. Fergus Slattery had not been fit in Paris because of a flu virus. Willie Duncan, his replacement at Cardiff and Twickenham, was clearly not the answer and, although

McGrath had the reputation of being the young Slattery, the prospect of McGrath playing his first international was less terrifying than that of Slattery in front of his home crowd playing what undoubtedly would have been his last. The Scots of course had seen McGrath in action in the B international at Melrose – a difficult afternoon for him because of the superiority of the Scottish forwards and half backs.

It was during the Irish visit to the Borders that the name of Sean McGaughey had cropped up. Not even the Irish could pass up a name like that and word of the Hawick flanker's exploits had filtered across the Irish Sea. But by then McGaughey had nailed his colours to the mast and, the day after Ireland's defeat at Twickenham, McGaughey was in the Scotland B side which gained a courageous 13–10 victory over the French at Albi. McGaughey, who had revelled in the close quarter combat that day, was taken from the field on a stretcher but, unsinkable, had returned from hospital to rejoin his teammates at the aftermatch celebration. Before the season was out McGaughey was to win a full cap, but how much Ireland could have done with his wholehearted commitment against Scotland at Lansdowne Road.

Playing in the same pack with McGaughey at Albi was Alister Campbell, another of Hawick's rising stars. Strong, mobile and fearless, Campbell had also played at Melrose and had been in the second row for the Whites in the Scottish trial. He was the obvious successor to Bill Cuthbertson in the Scotland side and when Cuthbertson aggravated the groin injury he had received during the Calcutta Cup and had to withdraw from the Irish game, it was Campbell who was brought in.

The Scottish party, as was now the custom before an away game, trained at Murrayfield on the Thursday afternoon. This was a productive session at which both Iain Paxton and Andy Irvine, who was a replacement, proved their fitness. Paxton had damaged knee ligaments

playing for Selkirk against Stewarts-Melville the previous Saturday and had, therefore, not played in a full game since the Calcutta Cup. But all the doubts were removed on Thursday and in the late

'Oot o' ma way Mossy'. Alister Campbell asserts his authority over Keane in his first international

We have lift off – Alan Tomes gets well above Donal Lenihan to win a lineout for Scotland

afternoon Paxton left, along with the rest of the squad, for the Scots' hideout in the foothills of the Dublin mountains at Kilternan.

They departed with the best wishes of a nation – the wishes of those, at any rate, who were not accompanying the team although there were times when it seemed as if the whole of Scotland had moved to Dublin for the weekend. The Irish, beguiling folk that they are, were at pains to assure the Scots that they would be rooting for a Scottish victory. 'That's as may be,' drawled Willie Duggan when he heard of this treason, 'but none of them will be wearing a green jersey on Saturday.'

Fergus Slattery and Tom Kiernan, the two major influences in Ireland's Triple Crown success in 1982, believed that the Scots would win. Kiernan praised the Scots for the exemplary manner in which they had upheld the traditions of the game over the years; Slattery felt that the Scots were much stronger in the key areas of the game at half back and in the back row. Both, however, felt that the biggest obstacle to a Scottish victory would be the Scots themselves. 'The crunch will come,' said Slattery, 'if they find themselves down at halftime.' Little did he know that by halftime the game would be over.

Dublin was a wild place to be on Friday. Gale-force winds and snow showers attended the Scots training on Friday morning. It was a lively hour-long session. Telfer and Aitken went to Lansdowne Road that afternoon noting carefully how forcibly the wind surged into the righthand corner on the old stand side. 'Just made for one of Roy Laidlaw's wee breaks,' remarked Aitken. But Telfer hoped that the storm would abate. He did not want to see a match of such importance reduced to a lottery. He recalled that it was on just such a day that Ireland had won the Triple Crown by beating Scotland two years previously. 'A game of two halves,' he remarked ruefully, 'with Ireland winning both of them.' But that was when Ollie Campbell was at his peak; there would be no Campbell this time.

Ireland were on the slippery slope: they had been forced to make changes. The problem was that the replacements were no better and in some cases a good deal worse than the men they replaced. There were rumours that the Irish, with nothing to lose, would treat the game as a festival

Be Jaysus! – first it was Laidlaw, now it's Hunter. Tony Doyle was hounded by both

Keith Robertson's try

and would throw caution to the winds. But the Scots would believe that when they saw it. Though the average age of the Irish pack had dropped since the French game at the beginning of the season, there remained a doubt about the forwards' stamina. A running game would not, therefore, be in the interests of the side. Moreover it would play right into the hands of the Scottish breakaways who had bewitched and bewildered better back divisions than the Irish. It was much more likely that the Irish would engage in their well-rehearsed war of attrition using all the experience that Duggan, Keane and company had at their disposal to wear down the Scots in the scrums and line-outs. Their efforts would be fuelled and supported by Tony Ward at out half.

The plan was straightforward – Ward would kick the forwards into attacking positions, Lenihan would win the line-outs and Ward would then kick the goals. Rutherford was the man the Irish feared the most. If Les Cusworth, who had opened all manner of doors on the Irish blind side at Twickenham, could find that amount of space what, they asked, would Rutherford do?

In his *Scotsman* preview, Chris Rea warned that the Irish would be foolish to ignore Roy Laidlaw, who that day would become Scotland's most capped scrum-half. 'Laidlaw, as he proved against Ireland and England last season, is without peer as a snapper-up of tries from quickly heeled scrummage ball. . . . There may therefore be more room for Laidlaw's quicksilver raids given that the excellence of the scrummage possession and superiority of the Scots' rucking can be maintained.' Like Laidlaw, Colin Deans would be breaking new ground in this game. He would become Scotland's most capped hooker and, although he would no doubt have relished the opportunity to have confronted Ciaran Fitzgerald who had kept him out of the Lions Test side, it was better that events had conspired against it. There were distractions enough to enliven the occasion without the additional pressure of a media-promoted private feud.

On the Friday night, the players watched a video provided by Jim Telfer. It was not a rerun of the dramatic draw against New Zealand or of the win at Cardiff, or even of the Calcutta Cup victory. Instead, it was the film of the South's humiliating defeat by the All Blacks. 'I showed you that,' said Telfer bluntly, 'because ten of you who played that day are playing tomorrow.'

Tomorrow dawned – bright and dry but despite a reduction in the wind it was still strong enough to be a significant factor. Having talked amongst themselves, the Scots decided that if they won the toss they would take the wind. The Irish, however, thought differently. Duggan won the toss and decided, as Scotland had done in similar conditions two years previously, to face the wind. Duggan's biggest mistake was to be on the losing side; had Ireland won, the decision to give Scotland first use of the wind would have been vindicated. As it was, the decision was the wrong one. It was not, however, Duggan's only mistake that afternoon. Jim Aitken led his team onto the field not knowing which end the Scots would be defending. He took his players to the side he would have chosen had he won the toss, but positioned close enough to the halfway line to effect a quick change after the Anthem had been played. He could not believe his luck when the Irish made no move to change ends as the bands marched off the field.

The referee was Fred Howard, an Englishman; like Owen Doyle at Cardiff, he was taking charge of his first international match. He had a reputation for being a stickler for the laws and, during the South of Scotland's tour to Ulster, had not taken at all kindly to remarks Aitken had made to him on the field. Aitken hoped fervently that he had forgotten the incident and in any case, the Scots had surely learned their lessons from the England game.

In the first half hour the Scots were much too busy scoring points to indulge in backchat with the referee. For the Scottish supporters, both those who had waited forty-six years for this moment and those who had not been born when Scotland had last won the Triple Crown, the opening 30 minutes seemed unreal. The ferocity of the Scottish forwards, Leslie's suicide missions into enemy territory, Rutherford's sublime kicking and, above all, Laidlaw's tour de force as the scrum-half, completely disarmed the Irish.

There were a couple of Irish spasms early in the second half, when Johnny Murphy kicked a penalty and converted Michael Kiernan's try, but at no stage did the Scots lose sight of their prize. Once again it was the tight five forwards who laid the foundations of the victory. The scrummage could be relied upon to provide quality possession and, in the line-out, Campbell, who made a most encouraging international debut, played his full part along with Paxton and Tomes whose two-handed take close to the Scottish line early in the second half was as crucial as any. Leslie, with Duggan and McGrath draped round his neck, nevertheless dominated at the tail of the line-out. At that stage in the international season it was clear that no other individual, save perhaps Gallion the French scrum-half, had been more important to his country than Leslie had been to Scotland. Once again the Scots scattered their opponents at the rucks. Ireland's most serious weakness was at half back where Doyle and Ward, who eventually limped from the field with a hip injury, possessed none of the harmony displayed by the Scottish halves. Doyle was hounded first by Laidlaw and then by Gordon Hunter, Laidlaw's replacement throughout the second half.

Laidlaw, however, had done more in one half than most players achieve in a lifetime. He burst forth with two sparkling tries, one from a ruck, the other from a quickly heeled scrummage ball. The first try after five minutes came from a line-out inside the Irish 22. Campbell took Paxton's tap down, peeled from the ruck, Laidlaw scampered blind, wrong-footed the Irish defence and forced his way over. Peter Dods, who converted Laidlaw's try, kicked two more penalties before the decisive score. A scrummage was awarded close to the Irish line. The Scots changed their pack formation in order to facilitate the wheel. Deans struck cleanly and the Scottish scrum began to roll forward towards the Irish line, turning as it did so. Suddenly Duggan was in the Scottish back row, Howard blew up and awarded a penalty try. The Irish were disbelieving, the Scots were in complete agreement with a decision which was marginal and, in the circumstances, extremely brave.

There is no doubt that Duggan deliberately foiled Scotland's attempts to go for the pushover and should certainly have been penalized; but whether a try would *probably* have followed is open to doubt. Whatever the whys and wherefores, Scotland gained six points instead of a possible three and Duggan, who was directly responsible for conceding another penalty from which Scotland scored later in the game, had not exactly played a captain's innings.

Before halftime Laidlaw was off and running again – this time from a scrum but once again through the flimsy Irish blind-side defence and into the same corner (which will evermore be known in Scotland as 'Roy's Corner'). Once the Scots had overcome Ireland's token resistance in the second half and once Hunter had found his feet in his first international, the Scots were home and hosed. The backs conjoined – Hunter made a diagonal break, fed Rutherford who broke through the gossamer defence and put Robertson in for Scotland's fourth try. The fifth was easily the best with the Scottish three-quarters sweeping the ball to the wing where Peter Dods had materialized to make the extra man.

The Scots had won the Triple Crown for the first time since 1938 and for the ninth time in their history. They had done it by winning two of their three legs away from home and what is more they had done it in style, their 32–9 victory being their highest ever score against Ireland.

7   The Grand Slam

After a wait of forty-six years no one at Lansdowne Road was going to deny the Scottish supporters, who had a mind to invade the pitch, their moment of glory. But it can be tiresome and even dangerous for the players. Struggling to reach the protective police cordon, Gordon Hunter collided with a supporter and, at the very moment of impact, feared the worst. Twice in the past he had fractured his cheek bone and now a freak accident had caused it to happen for a third time. He would be out of rugby for at least six weeks which would certainly deprive him of a cap against France in the event of Laidlaw being unfit, and could even jeopardize his chances of going with Scotland to Rumania at the end of the season. But that night, during the subdued revelry, Hunter took the philosophical and eminently sensible view that whatever else had befallen him, he had at least won his first cap after three years as a replacement, and that there were not many Scots who could claim to have played in a Triple Crown winning side.

Nevertheless, there was grave concern in the Scottish camp. Laidlaw had taken a knock during the first half against Ireland and had left the field suffering from migraine which had impaired his vision. He was apparently prone to these attacks and so it was decided that he should undergo a full examination. Laidlaw had been playing rugby almost uninterrupted since winning his first cap against Ireland in 1980. He had played in twenty-six consecutive internationals for Scotland. He had toured France, Australia and New Zealand with his country and had been to New

Zealand with the Lions the previous summer. During that tour, he had taken a fearful pounding without so much as a murmur of complaint at his forwards, a number of whom, had they a fraction of Laidlaw's heart, might have earned the right to call themselves Lions. Laidlaw returned fatigued both mentally and physically and, until the Scottish trial, had played like a man half expecting a ton of All Black beef to descend on him at any moment. It was against this background that Laidlaw was to be medically examined and, in the light of results, a decision would be taken on his fitness for the French game. One thing was certain, the final decision would not rest with the player.

In the meantime the selectors were left with a perplexing choice should the tests prove that Laidlaw was unfit. There were three candidates. Douglas Morgan, Stuart Johnston and Dave Bryson. Morgan had won the last of his twenty-one caps in 1978 and had announced that he would be retiring from the game at the end of the season. Johnston, the younger brother of David, had displayed considerable potential behind the lightweight Watsonian pack. He was durable and audacious, qualities without which no good scrum-half can ever hope to become a better one. In style and attitude he was, therefore, the closest to Laidlaw and despite Morgan's massive experience, the selectors' probable choice should Laidlaw fail his medical. The third candidate, Gala's Dave Bryson, the former Scotland B cap, had at various times sat on the replacements bench for Scotland, but his representative career

Bravo mon ami. Jérôme Gallion, the pulse of the French side, scores against England. Peter Wheeler kneels in surrender

had been overshadowed by both Laidlaw and Hunter.

The selectors announced an unchanged side for France leaving a vacancy at scrum-half. At the weekend they would be at three venues: at Inverleith where Morgan's Stewarts-Melville were playing Boroughmuir, at Burnbrae to see how Johnston fared against the once mighty West of Scotland, and at Kilmarnock where Bryson was turning out for Gala. In the meantime Laidlaw had undergone his tests and had fully satisfied his examiners. There had been no question of a concussion at Lansdowne Road and there was no correlation between the knock he received during the game and the migraine. He was 100 per cent fit and all Scotland rejoiced. Morgan, Johnston and Bryson heard the news before they took the field for their respective games. It would not, after all, be the starring role they were playing for but the position as Laidlaw's understudy and it was Johnston, after a typically pugnacious perform-

ance at Burnbrae, who was summoned to the bench for the grand finale at Murrayfield.

The French, meanwhile, announced the same side as the one that had finished the game against England in Paris. Like Scotland at Lansdowne Road, France had scored five tries that day but during the game had lost their lock forward, Alain Lorieux. He had been replaced by Jean Charles Orso, whose arrival had coincided with a marked

One loose ball that the French couldn't kill

What have I done to deserve this? Pierre Berbizier, the replacement for Gallion, tries to cut off Leslie's determined run

improvement in the French scrummaging. By common consent, France were considered to be the best side in the championship. The return of Jérôme Gallion at scrum-half had brought renewed heart to the forwards and had unleashed the full force of the fastest back division in international rugby. Only the volatile French could shun a player of Gallion's class for three years. But now the petty squabbling was at an end, the hatchets had been buried somewhere other than in Gallion's back and France were much the richer for his presence. The pack had also been stiffened since the start of the season. Garuet and Cremaschi had been replaced by Dospital, an experienced loose head, and Dubroca who, although he was no Paparemborde, could be relied upon to look after himself. Orso and Condom were the workhorses in the second row, Joinel was still in the top flight of back row forwards and Jean-Pierre Rives, if a slightly faded version of the flaxen-haired fury of past seasons, was nevertheless an inspirational and charismatic leader. Behind the forwards lurked Jean-Patrick Lescarboura whose precision as a goal kicker had earned him the nickname of the 'executioner'. In his three previous championship games he had scored 46 points, a new French record, and only 6 short of Ollie Campbell's record for an entire season.

The Irish, Welsh and English had all returned from their confrontations with France convinced that if the speed and guile of Estève, Blanco, Codorniou and Gallion didn't succeed then the accuracy of Lescarboura most assuredly would. Wheeler, the England captain, had described them as 'unbeatable', the Welsh raved about the centre pairing of Codorniou and Sella, and Jean Piqué, who coached the French backs and who had played his rugby in the heady company of the Boniface brothers, was convinced that this was the best back division France had ever fielded. The pack was undoubtedly the strongest since the Grand Slam winning side of 1977.

Incredibly, two days before the match, the selectors decided to dismantle it. Dominique Erbani, their flank forward and a decidedly useful customer at number 5 in the line-out, went down with flu. There was no replacement loose forward in the party but a host of capable players in France, the most obvious being Pierre Lacans of Béziers. But why settle for one change when you can make five? Why not switch Joinel from number 8, where he had been playing superbly, to the flank, move Orso, whose scrummaging had so impressed England, from the second row to number 8, and call up Francis Haget, who was

thirty-four and had only recently resumed his rugby career after a two-year break? *C'est bon – non?* Only two minor alterations to make now: Haget and Condom would have to switch sides in the scrummage and, of course, change their numbers.

C'était chaotique! Haget was nowhere fit enough to play a game of such pace and passion and Orso, despite the fact that he was no stranger to the

Paxton first to the ball

I reckon we've got one good eye between us, ref.
Peter Dods surveys the damage to Winston Jones

refereeing in his first international. Jim Telfer accepted the fact that technically the French were the best equipped side in the championship. He knew that Gallion would present many more problems for the Scottish back row than either Youngs or Doyle had done in the two previous games. He also was aware that France was adept at killing the rucks, the one area where the Scots could claim absolute superiority. But his last words to his side were cautionary ones – 'discipline at all times'.

The skies were forbidding on the day of the match but the conditions were perfect and Murrayfield has seldom been more colourful for an occasion which, win or lose, the Scots were determined to enjoy. At worst it would be a celebration of the Triple Crown, at best it would be Scotland's finest hour since 1925 when they had last won the Grand Slam. One patriot had flown all the way from Sydney especially for the match. The whole country waited, watched and listened. The halftime score from Murrayfield was relayed to a host of soccer grounds from Aberdeen to Stranraer – Scotland 3 France 6.

The bare facts told nothing of a half of almost stupefying intensity in which the French backs had looked like the world beaters we were told they were, and drew superlatives from those French commentators who had been following the game for thirty years or more. More ominous, however, was the power of the French scrummage which, at one point, threatened to sweep the Scots over their own goal line. Apart from the briefest respite during that pulsating opening quarter – when Orso was penalized in front of his posts and Dods kicked the penalty – the Scots were trapped in their own half. French confidence grew. Their three-quarters, steeply banked, swooped down on the Scottish line. Estève went off on a blazing run down the left, while Begu's cross kick from the right had the Scottish defence in a desperate tangle. French appeals for a score on that occasion, dismissed by Winston Jones, hardly seemed to matter. A try must come. Sure enough

position, was not fast enough for an international number 8. The balance of the French pack had been fatally disturbed.

The Scots, ignoring this Gallic version of musical chairs, concentrated on their own game plan. They knew that they must draw the steam from the French in the scrummage and somehow outmanoeuvre them in the line-out. But they would have to tread warily because the line-out was Winston Jones's speciality. Jones, like Owen Doyle and Frank Howard before him, would be

– Lescarboura's diagonal to the Scottish line was partially stopped by Baird and tidied up by Leslie, but from the scrummage Orso picked up and ran blind, and Gallion from a few yards out was unstoppable. But Lescarboura's conversion, far from settling the French, had the opposite effect. They became moody and introverted. Lescarboura kicked and kicked badly. The more he kicked with his three-quarters fretting outside him, the more inaccurate he became.

With their spirits rising, the Scots rallied round a couple of explosive bursts by Leslie and finished the half in good heart. They knew that their position could have been very much worse. In the

Dead-eye Dods kicks another goal

58

A wise decision by Blanco

ten minutes before halftime, they had begun to
exert some pressure in the scrummage. Iain Milne
was putting the squeeze on Dospital, Haget was
visibly wilting and Rives was too busy arguing
with the referee to take stock of the situation.
Captaining his country for the thirty-second time,
Rives can scarcely ever have made a worse job of
it. He seemed powerless to prevent indiscipline
from spreading through the ranks. Indeed he
himself did much to foster it. His tactical

appreciation was clouded as a result. The
line-outs were going badly for the French. Haget
was a spent force long before halftime, Condom
had no pretensions as a jumper and even the
splendid Joinel suffered from the *mal de la touche*
which ultimately broke them. Yet Rives remained
blind to the need to reduce the line-out to two,
three or even four men.

The supreme folly of the French, however, was
the abandonment of the flowing rugby of the first

twenty minutes and their surrender to baser instincts. Within two minutes of the game starting, when they were penalized at successive line-outs, they should have deduced that, for the remainder of the game, cleanliness was going to be every bit as important to them as godliness.

Their supplications to Mr Jones went unheeded and their intemperance was punished by Peter Dods, who displayed an inner calm conspicuously lacking in the French temperament. Not only did he overcome the physical handicap of having his right eye partially closed for most of the game, he

The loss of Gallion – the last straw for France

Roy Laidlaw evades John Scott, whose jersey is caught on a Scottish fingernail

The bear hug – Winterbottom is flattened by Iain Milne

Roy Laidlaw wrongfoots the Irish defence on his way to scoring at Lansdowne Road

Never mind the ball – get on with the game. Alister Campbell plays gooseberry to Des Fitzgerald and Iain Paxton, while Duggan appears to be overcome by nausea

The hours of practice have
paid off – John Rutherford's
two-footed mastery was one
of the features of Scotland's
Grand Slam season

Gallion and Sella are too late
to block Keith Robertson's
carefully weighted chip.
Rutherford hangs back in case
of an emergency

It took two
Frenchmen to do
it, but Leslie
appears to have
lost this one

Calder's Grand Slam try – Aitken rejoices, but Winston Jones seems uncertain

recovered from the mental trauma of missing two apparently crucial goal kicks just after halftime. He finished with five penalties and the conversion of Jim Calder's late try for a total of 17 points which equalled the Scottish record held by Andy Irvine. Furthermore, his total of 50 points in the championship season beat the previous best of 35 also set by Irvine.

Immediately after the two lapses by Dods, Lescarboura increased the French lead to 6 points with a penalty. Dods replied with two crisply struck penalties of his own before Lescarboura's massive drop goal restored France's lead and took the Frenchman to a new points record for a championship season. But by now the French were close to disintegration. Their irrita-

tion with the referee had reached the point of open hostility. They were enraged by the frequency with which he took up a position on their side of the line-out, by his failure to punish the Scots' three-quarters and loose forwards for offside and above all by the imbalance of the penalties awarded in the first half hour – nine to Scotland, none to France. Here they could justifiably feel aggrieved. Very few sides having to withstand the kind of pressure that the Scots were being subjected to could survive for so long without conceding a penalty. Yet according to Mr Jones's reading of the situation, the Scots were paragons of virtue. As the French fumed, the Scots got on with the game.

The last straw was the loss of Gallion in the

second half. Racing round the back of a line-out he was knocked unconscious in a collision with Leslie and replaced by Pierre Berbizier, who was an experienced international scrum-half but lacked Gallion's commanding presence and possessed none of his flair. Even before Gallion had departed the Scots had begun to assert their authority.

Telfer, for once breaking his rule of silence in such matters, afterwards singled out Milne as the outstanding and most influential Scot. Everyone, including those cyclonic furies in the back row, Leslie and Calder, knew that without the collective grit of the tight forwards there would have been no Triple Crown, no Grand Slam. Aitken and Milne, whose labours had so often gone

unnoticed in the front row were never bested during the season. In the French game Colin Deans had outplayed Dintrans, the one man who might have challenged his status as the world's best hooker. In the second row Tomes, Campbell and Cuthbertson had bristled with aggressiveness, disputing every scrum, every line-out, every ruck and every maul. It was fitting, therefore, that their indispensable contributions should have been acknowledged just as it was appropriate that the try which won the Grand Slam should have been scored by a member of the crack unit that was Scotland's back row. A line-out close to the French line, a misdirected tap down from the luckless Joinel and Calder, the arch opportunist, scored the try which brought a nation to its feet.

8 Conclusions

We've done it! The Triple Crown at last

As any astrologer worth his salt will tell you, Scotland's stars were all in ascendancy throughout 1983–84. There cannot be the slightest doubt that the Scots enjoyed their share of good fortune, although one critic's dismissal of their success as a 'travesty' was grossly unfair. There has not been a Grand Slam won yet which has not owed something to luck, but Grand Slams are not won by luck alone.

It helped, of course, that the Welsh selectors, still in a state of shock following the Rumanian defeat, made a pig's breakfast of their side for the Scottish game in January: that Bob Norster, in a moment of sheer madness, ran a penalty at a crucial time when three points beckoned, and that Owen Doyle, the referee, gave the Scots the benefit of at least one doubtful pass in the build-up to Paxton's try. It helped, of course, when Dusty Hare missed kick after kick in the Calcutta Cup and Willie Duggan gave Scotland the wind at Lansdowne Road. And who would deny that the French were technically the best equipped side in the championship? But what did that matter when, temperamentally, they were the worst?

Were not Scotland's doggedness and grit more worthy of a championship? Mostly, the Scots were masters of their own destiny. They had in Adam Robson, their President, a man whose love of his country was equalled only by his passion for rugby; whose modesty and humility, even at the moment of Scotland's supreme triumph, set an example which was followed by Jim Aitken and his players. The selectors, under the convenorship of Ian MacGregor, had worked painstakingly over a number of years to build up a squad capable of sustaining a challenge over four games. They had done it – and it is important that this is understood in Scotland – they had done it despite a domestic organization which is not properly structured to produce the best possible international XV. Three arduous tours to France, New Zealand and Australia in successive seasons were of greater benefit to the selectors than an overloaded league system and an ill-defined district championship stripped of any status.

In Jim Telfer, Scotland had a man of the unimpeachable integrity, who had promised before he went to New Zealand that he would coach the national side for another season and, though he cannot have relished the prospect on his return from the Lions tour, he kept his word. Throughout the season he used the knowledge and the lessons learned in New Zealand to maximum advantage. He cajoled, pleaded and, for the most part, bullied his players; one only had to look at the changing attitude and the application of those Borderers, who one week had been

crushed at Netherdale and the next came within the width of a post of beating New Zealand, to realize the extent of Telfer's influence. 'We feared Jim more than we did the All Blacks,' said one. More important, however, they respected him. Without that Tom Smith would not perhaps have transformed himself from dormouse to dragon within a fortnight, nor would Iain Milne have put himself through such a punishing routine to win the deserved praise and admiration of his coach. What was it that fuelled Alan Tomes as he rocketed above Ireland's Donal Lenihan in the line-out? What was it that put the steel into Paxton's game? There were many reasons, no doubt, but Telfer was the catalyst.

He was also something of a psychologist, to wit his screening of the South's abject surrender on the eve of the Irish game. He was a strict disciplinarian. Following the Triple Crown victory in Dublin, the team were scheduled to appear on a television programme and Telfer was concerned that the players put over the correct image. It was at his insistence that they were smartly turned out and that they conducted themselves in a dignified manner.

Jim Aitken, like his coach, was a hard man to please. He and Telfer both knew at the start of the season that Scotland's Achilles heel was the line-out. Bill Cuthbertson and Alister Campbell were both hard, driving forwards but neither was a recognized line-out specialist. Nor was Alan Tomes a main line jumper. But throughout the season, Scotland's greatest virtue was the ability to cover up their deficiencies. Against Wales the line-out weaknesses were never exposed, largely as a result of Tomes's spoiling, Leslie's jumping, Deans's throwing and Moriarty's disorientation. In the tight, Aitken, Deans and Milne were masters in their own house and very often masters in their opponents' as well. Their scrummaging was crucial in the games against New Zealand, England and France, especially so in the Calcutta Cup when Milne put such pressure on Colin White that it unbalanced England's drive.

We'll support you ever more

If the back row and half backs played the starring roles in Scotland's glorious season – and there was no better pivot five in the championship – then it was the front five's refusal to submit to any opponent which provided them with their platform. There was also a responsive and, when the need arose, resourceful three-quarter line and a full back, unobtrusive and unassuming, who kicked his goals, held his catches and missed no tackles. Peter Dods and Serge Blanco, the respective full backs of Scotland and France, perfectly illustrated Bill Dickinson's point made before that breathless decider: 'Both teams have proved that they can attack and can score points, but the victors today will be the team with the greater appetite for defence.' Dods, with one eye closed, the other glinting fiercely, stood his ground on one side. On the other was the sublimely gifted Blanco who, when he had discovered early in the second half that this was to be a dour fight and not a dazzling fête, had lost interest.

This indomitable spirit, personified by Dods, was fundamental to Scotland's second Grand Slam. That it happened last season surprised others more than it did the Scottish squad who had been working patiently and with no little confidence towards the ultimate goal. By reaching it the Scots had done themselves, their country and the game of rugby, proud.

The end of the road. Aitken besieged by autograph hunters after Scotland's first Grand Slam for 59 years.

9 The Players

J AITKEN (Gala) captain. Loose head prop. Born 22.11.47 in Penicuik. 5'11". 15st 9lbs. 24 caps. The determination with which Jim Aitken set about repairing an unsatisfactory academic record at school to become managing director of a flourishing grain and agricultural machinery company has also carried him to the position of Scotland's most successful post-war captain. Aitken twice considered retirement in the twelve months before the Grand Slam but he had the good sense and foresight to change his mind on each occasion. He was first capped at the age of twenty-nine against England in 1977 and, though he lost his place to Gerry McGuinness on the Australian tour in 1982, he returned to the side the following season and assumed the captaincy in the game against England at Twickenham. In his seven games as captain, Aitken had been defeated only once – against Rumania in Bucharest. He has been nicknamed 'Big Daddy' partly because at the age of thirty-six he was the oldest player in the championship last season and partly because of the paternal interest he takes in his players. A mutual respect and understanding has developed between Jim Telfer, the coach, and Aitken, who admits to being very much his own man. He has captained his club to a division one championship, has led the South to the inter-district title and is the first player from a Border club to lead Scotland to the Triple Crown. His one and only international try was the decisive one against Wales at Cardiff last season. NZ. W. E. I. F.

P W DODS (Gala). Full back. Born 6.1.58 in Gala. 5'8". 11st 10lbs. 10 caps. In many ways Peter Dods was given the most unenviable task in Scottish rugby when he was called into the national side in 1983 to replace the injured Andy Irvine at full back. But in his quiet, unassuming way, Dods has made the position his own and is the second highest scorer in Scotland's history. In last season's championship, he set a new Scottish individual points-scoring record, his 50 points breaking the previous record of 35 held by Irvine, and in major internationals to date has scored 113 points. Without Irvine's speed or his ability to run at opponents from deep defensive positions, Dods nevertheless gets himself into scoring positions, his try in the game against Rumania being one of the finest of the international season. A joiner by trade, Dods is something of a rarity in the Gala side in that he was actually born in the town. Dods began his rugby career on the wing but was switched to full back in the Gala Wanderers side when the original selection failed to turn up. He won four B caps, toured with Scotland to France, New Zealand and Australia – on the latter trip finishing top scorer with 54 points. He is the sixth Gala player to occupy the full-back position for Scotland. NZ. W. E. I. F.

S MUNRO (Ayr). Right wing. Born 11.6.58 in Ayr. 5'11". 13st 2lbs. 10 caps. An international career which began against Ireland in 1980 has since been blighted by injury and for Steve Munro last season brought yet more disappointment. Selected for the games against New Zealand and England he was forced to withdraw from both because of injury and ended up playing in only one game – against Wales. His progress to full international status was by way of Scottish Schools, whom he represented in one of the rare victories over Wales in 1976, and Scotland B, for whom he played in the wins against Ireland and France in 1979. Whilst there has never been any doubt about Munro's strength, speed and ability, he has occasionally lacked the lethal finishing power that one expects from a player so physically well-endowed.

J A POLLOCK (Gosforth). Right wing. Born 16.11.58 in Newcastle-upon-Tyne. 5'11". 12st 5lbs. 7 caps. Whether or not Jim Pollock was born lucky or had good luck thrust upon him is not at all certain. It is, however, undeniably the case that Pollock has made the most of it; one eminent critic even went so far as to suggest that in the event of his being dropped from the national side, he should be taken along to the game as a mascot and set down, swathed in navy blue and white, on the half way line. His extraordinary tale began on the eve of the Welsh game at Cardiff in 1982 when he came into the side as a last minute replacement for Keith Robertson, the victim of a throat infection. During that unforgettable afternoon, Pollock scored one of Scotland's five tries in their 34–18 victory. He then played in the winning side at Twickenham, one of only two victorious Scottish sides on that ground since the war, and was called in to replace Steve Munro for last season's first international – against New Zealand. It was Pollock's try which saved the game. Educated at the Royal Grammar School, Newcastle, Pollock received his early grounding game from John Elders, the former England coach, and played for Northumberland in their County Championship winning year. But his Scottish connections are impeccable. His father is a former pupil of George Heriots and a member of Preston Lodge. In his seven internationals, he has only once been on the losing side. NZ. E(R). I. F.

The lucky mascot. Jim Pollock kicks to touch against France

D I JOHNSTON (Watsonians). Centre. Born 20.10.58 in Edinburgh. 5′9″. 10st 7lbs. 22 caps. Although he flirted with the idea of extending his career as a professional soccer player, and may well have had the ability to succeed in that competitive arena, David Johnston instead decided to return to the rugby fold. Having received his tuition at Watsons College and playing for Scottish Schools, he turned his attention to soccer. He was wooed by, among others, Rangers, signed for Hibernian and was later transferred to Hearts. His career as a professional footballer, interrupted by injury, lasted eighteen months. He first played for Edinburgh in 1978 and won his cap the following year against New Zealand. In his twenty-two appearances for Scotland he has scored four tries – two against Ireland, one against Wales (which owed everything to his power of acceleration), and one last season against England in which he displayed all the close control of a professional soccer player. NZ. W. E. I. F.

K W ROBERTSON (Melrose). Centre or wing. Born 5.12.54 in Hawick. 5′11″. 11st. 27 caps. In common with many who are versatile enough to play anywhere in the back division, Keith Robertson's skills have often been underrated. He has played twenty times for his country on the wing, seven in the centre and has scored five tries and two drop goals in major internationals. Robertson has twice overcome serious shoulder injuries to regain his place in the national side. He dislocated his shoulder in Scotland's game against the Barbarians at the end of 1983 and last season sprang a collar bone which kept him out of the internationals against New Zealand and Wales. He has a fine positional sense, a marvellously adhesive pair of hands and is defensively sound. He is also a thoroughly popular and inveterate tourist, having travelled with Scotland to the Far East, France, Australia and Rumania. E. F.

The versatile Keith Robertson

A complete footballer. John Rutherford confirmed his status as a player of the highest class

A E KENNEDY (Watsonians). Centre. Born 30.7.54 in Edinburgh. 6'5". 14st. 3 caps. For Euan Kennedy the final step into the international side was the hardest. He had been so close for so long both as a full back and as a centre. He had progressed through all the normal channels from district to the national under-21 side to Scotland B, whom he captained to victory over France in 1981, and finally to the senior side in a Scottish trial. Yet the final honour always eluded him and at the age of twenty-nine he seemed destined to be lumped along with so many others as a first-class player at club and minor representative levels unable to make the transition to full international status. But Kennedy's chance came last season against the All Blacks. He played well for Edinburgh against the tourists alongside David Johnston, in the centre, and when Keith Robertson withdrew with a shoulder injury, Kennedy was the obvious replacement. Uncompromising in the tackle, Kennedy also had the ability to stand upright in the face of the All Blacks' attacks. He did the job required of him and was retained for the games against Wales and England, the latter an occasion of wickedly contrasting fortunes. Having scored one of Scotland's two tries he then tore knee ligaments and was replaced by Jim Pollock. He was encased in plaster for the next six weeks and missed Scotland's Triple Crown-winning game in Dublin and the Grand Slam decider against France. NZ. W. E.

G R T BAIRD (Kelso). Wing. Born 12.4.60 in Kelso. 5'9". 12st. 16 caps. Into every life a little rain must fall and if Roger Baird's Grand Slam season fell someway short of expectations it is surely a temporary setback in what has been a glittering rugby career. First capped at the age of twenty-one and a British Lion in New Zealand two seasons later, he returned from that tour as one of the very few successes. He played in eleven of the eighteen matches including all four Tests, and scored one of the two Lions' tries in the Test series. In his first season in international rugby, he startled the Welsh in Cardiff with a dazzling break from his own line, thus beginning the move which ended with Jim Calder's try. But last season he displayed indifferent form. His defensive alignment was poor and he was beaten several times in international matches by opposing wings. This may in part have been due to the fact that his club Kelso played him for most of the season in the centre and on occasions at stand-off. His confidence wavered although never his enthusiasm and, in the Calcutta Cup, his harassing of Dusty Hare was one of the features of the game. It has been another criticism of him that, in his fifteen consecutive internationals, he has yet to score a try although in fairness this says more about Scotland's tactics than about Baird's abilities as a try scorer. On the Lions tour he finished as top try scorer with six and has scored twenty-two tries in thirty-seven appearances for the South. Educated at St Mary's, Melrose and Merchiston, he played scrum-half for the Scottish Schools and once won three Border sprint titles in the one afternoon. NZ. W. E. I. F.

J Y RUTHERFORD (Selkirk). Stand-off. Born 4.10.55 in Selkirk. 6'1". 12st. 28 caps. 'Some day John Rutherford will realize just how good a player he really is.' So said Barry John after Scotland had beaten Wales at Cardiff in 1982. It is doubtful if even yet Rutherford has realized his full potential although his conviction during the Lions tour that Scotland had nothing to fear from the home countries in the international championship played a vital part in building morale. Last season his qualities as a runner were less in evidence than his uncanny accuracy as a kicker. There was no finer exhibition of this than his display against England. First capped against Wales in 1979, Rutherford is now Scotland's most capped stand-off and in his twenty-three appearances in partnership with Roy Laidlaw equalled the world record for a half-back partnership set by Barry John and Gareth Edwards. In 1981–82 Rutherford scored in each of the five internationals in which he played and, in all, has scored six tries and seven drop goals for Scotland. Educated at Selkirk High School, Rutherford works as an executive for a building society. NZ. W. E. I. F.

R J LAIDLAW (Jedforest). Scrum-half. Born 5.10.53 in Jedburgh. 5'7". 11st 7lbs. 28 caps. There is no more courageous and durable player than Roy Laidlaw. He is Scotland's most capped scrum-half, his twenty-eight caps having been won consecutively. He was, by force of circumstances, overplayed by the Lions in New Zealand, but by the start of the international championship had regained his form and was one of the most crucial elements in Scotland's success. His tireless covering in defence, his willingness to take on opposing forwards, the astuteness of his kicking and of course his two tries against Ireland epitomized the Scottish spirit. Laidlaw was awarded his first cap against Ireland in 1980 after playing in seven B internationals and thirteen times acting as international replacement. He had captained his club, district and country, and is one of the most widely travelled members of the side having toured the Far East, Argentina, Australia, France and New Zealand. NZ. W. E. I. F.

Roy Laidlaw – rejuvenated after a testing Lions tour in New Zealand. His form was one of the keys to Scotland's success

I G HUNTER (Selkirk). Scrum-half. Born 7.8.58 in Hawick. 5'10". 12st 4lbs. 1 cap. A summer spent improving his passing technique helped Gordon Hunter to begin last season with renewed confidence. He played with massive assurance in the early part of the season culminating in a superb display in the emphatic victory against Ireland in the B international at Melrose. As a result of his displays, he was selected for the South and for the Blues XV in the Scottish trial ahead of Roy Laidlaw. He was unable, however, to sustain his form. Laidlaw was first choice for Scotland's six internationals last season and, by the time Hunter eventually won his cap – coming on for the injured Laidlaw at Lansdowne Road – he had broken Laidlaw's own record of thirteen appearances on the replacements bench. Always with an eye for the break, Hunter paved the way for Keith Robertson's try against Ireland. A pupil of the Royal High School in Edinbrugh, he captained Scottish Schools against France and Ireland in 1975 and joined Selkirk the following year. He made his district debut for the South in 1980, and in 1983 captained Scotland B against France B. He has toured with Scotland to New Zealand, where he suffered a cheek bone fracture, to Australia and to Rumania. I(R).

C T DEANS (Hawick). Hooker. Born 3.5.55 in Hawick. 5'10". 13st 4lbs. 34 caps. Despite the fact that it has been said many times and in many ways, it is worth repeating that Colin Deans is the outstanding player in his position in world rugby; his supremacy both as a hooker and in the loose was proved beyond all doubt in the Grand Slam decider against the formidable Frenchman, Phillipe Dintrans. Critics of Deans have frequently pointed to his exuberance in the loose as proof that he has not been doing his duties in the tight but, in his six years as his country's hooker and in many worse packs than the one Scotland fielded last season, Deans has never failed in this area of play. Also an accomplished thrower in at the line-out he gave the finest demonstration of this skill at Cardiff last season. Since he was first capped against France in 1978, Deans has missed only three internationals: two through injury and one against Rumania at the end of last season because he was unavailable for the tour. He is Scotland's most capped hooker, was a member of the 1983 Lions side in New Zealand and has been a regular member of the South since 1974. He has scored one international try – against New Zealand in 1981. NZ. W. E. I. F.

The best hooker in the world. Colin Deans made his point in Scotland's colours last season

I G MILNE (Heriots FP). Tight-head prop. Born 17.6.58 in Edinburgh. 6'. 16st 5lbs. 24 caps. When Jim Telfer singled out Iain Milne for a special mention at the end of the French game, it was in recognition of Milne's dedication and devotion to duty. Milne's contribution had been immense, a fact which Telfer and the rest of the squad felt should be recorded. There can be no doubt that Milne's presence was greatly missed during the Rumanian tour. Educated at Heriots School and Heriot Watt University, Milne was first brought into the national squad at the relatively tender age for a prop of twenty and, a year later, won his first cap against Ireland. For one of his bulk, Milne can be remarkably light on his feet and it was from one of his line-out surges that Jim Aitken scored his try against Wales. But Milne's finest hour was undoubtedly his display against France, where his supremacy over the French loose head, Pierre Dospital, was one of the most significant factors in Scotland's victory. One of the eight Scots in the 1983 Lions tour to New Zealand, he was rated the number one tight head in the party by no less an authority than the All Blacks skipper Andy Dalton. A former captain of his club, Milne plays in the Heriots front row along with his two brothers, David and Kenneth. NZ. W. E. I. F.

A J CAMPBELL (Hawick). Lock. Born 1.1.59 in Hawick. 6'4". 16st 2lbs. 3 caps. There were times when it seemed that Alister Campbell's career would be hindered by his own versatility. His club, Hawick, could not make up their minds whether or not he served them best as a lock or a number 8 and, midway through the season when Derek Turnbull returned to the side, they mistakenly employed him in the latter position. But Campbell is best suited to the second row where the national selectors saw him as the heir apparent to Bill Cuthbertson. Still only twenty-five he has waited a long time for the chance which came last season against Ireland. He made his debut for Hawick in 1977 as an eighteen-year-old and the following year was a Scottish trialist. Last season he played impressively for the B side against Ireland at Melrose and against France at Albi and was called into the international side for the Triple Crown game against Ireland when Cuthbertson withdrew because of injury. He played well enough to be retained for the French game and was selected for the Rumanian tour where he won his third cap. Already he has displayed all the qualities which should ensure a long and successful international career. Educated at Hawick High School, he had been a regular member of the South for whom he has played both at lock and as a number 8 since 1981. I. F.

W CUTHBERTSON (Harlequins). Lock. Born 6.12.49 in Kilwinning. 6'3". 15st 7lbs. 20 caps. Having been with Scotland through the bad times, it seemed particularly unfortunate that this great-hearted player should miss a huge chunk of the good, but he did at least have the satisfaction of playing in two of Scotland's championship-winning sides against Wales and England. In the latter he injured a groin and was replaced by John Beattie. The injury failed to respond to treatment and he was forced to miss the Irish game. With the selectors understandably remaining loyal to the Triple Crown-winning side he therefore missed the French game as well. But Cuthbertson's value has never been underestimated and there are those in influential places who believe him to be the best rucking forward produced by Scotland for many a long year. His ability in this sphere was never seen to better advantage than against the All Blacks when Scotland out-rucked the best ruckers in the world. Cuthbertson is also invaluable in his role as protector and sweeper at the line-out. Nicknamed 'Gulliver' because of his hatred of flying, Cuthbertson won his first cap at the age of thirty. He received his schooling at Marr College and won his first cap from Kilmarnock before moving last season to Harlequins. He has played for Glasgow and the Anglo-Scots and has captained both. NZ. W. E.

A J TOMES (Hawick). Lock. Born 6.11.51 in Hawick. 6'5". 17st. 38 caps. Alan Tomes, who came into the national side for the Calcutta Cup match in 1976, is now four short of equalling Alastair McHarg's record number of caps for a Scottish lock. There have been times during these eight years when he may have appeared to lack the necessary urgency but he has proved to be one of the most durable of international forwards and, last season, played as well as he has ever done for his country. This was especially evident in the matches against England and Ireland where he took on two of the best jumpers in the country in Bainbridge and Lenihan and beat them. His season began inauspiciously. Having lost his international place the previous season he was dropped by the South selectors and left out of the Scottish side for the international against New Zealand. A member of the Whites pack in the trial, he regained his international place for the game against Wales and was immovable for the remainder of the season. Tomes, who played his early rugby with Gateshead Fell, was easily the most experienced member of last season's Scottish side having toured with the Barbarians to Canada, with Scotland to New Zealand twice, to the Far East and to Australia and with the 1980 Lions to South Africa. He has scored three tries in major internationals, two against Wales and one against England. W. E. I. F.

T J SMITH (Gala). Lock. Born 31.8.53 in East Lothian. 6′7″. 17st 12lbs. 2 caps. Along with Steve Munro, Tom Smith was surely the unluckiest player in Scottish rugby last season. Denied a cap in 1981 through injury when he had an outstanding trial in the senior side, he won his first cap against England at Twickenham two years later and scored a try in Scotland's 22–12 win. Last season he played impressively in the international against the All Blacks and seemed certain to keep his place for the remainder of the season. But a knee injury sustained while playing for the South against the Anglo-Scots in an inter-district game before Christmas set him back and he was passed over in favour of Alan Tomes for the first championship match against Wales. Tomes held on to his place throughout the season. Smith, who played for the B side in 1980 and 1981, rejected rugby in favour of basketball when he left school, winning 26 Scottish caps in that sport, before returning to the game in 1979. NZ.

J H CALDER (Stewarts-Melville FP). Flanker. Born 20.8.57 in Haddington. 6′. 14st 10lbs. 23 caps. Jim Calder was brought into the Scottish side in 1981, charged with the specific responsibility of stiffening the defences on the lefthand side of the scrummage. It had until then been the area most vulnerable to opposition attack but, since his arrival, Scotland's defensive play has improved immeasurably. Until the Rumanian tour, which Calder missed, he had played twenty-three games in a row and has formed an exceptional back-row partnership with David Leslie and Iain Paxton, Calder's support play complementing the qualities of the other two. He and his brother Finlay became the first twins to tour with Scotland when they went to Australia in 1982 and, in the club pack, they are joined by their other two brothers – John and Gavin. All four were schoolboy internationalists and John subsequently joined Jim and Finlay as a replacement in Australia. It is hard to think of an occasion when Calder has played a poor game for Scotland. He found Mark Douglas, the Welsh scrum-half, a difficult opponent at Cardiff but Scotland's defensive problems that day were sorted out by the time they played England, a game in which Calder was in superlative form. He played seven games for the Lions in New Zealand, including the Third Test in Dunedin where he broke his thumb and took no further part in the tour. He was educated at Knox Academy, Melville College and Heriot Watt University and has played district rugby in Edinburgh's colours since 1978. NZ. W. E. I. F.

David Leslie – the outstanding player in the Five Nations Championship

D G LESLIE (Gala). Flanker. Born 14.4.52 in Dundee. 6'1". 14st 7lbs. 29 caps. David Leslie's contention that he played just as well as a seventeen-year-old in the Glenalmond 1st XV as he did last season may well be true but his form certainly attracted less public attention and admiration at school than it did throughout Scotland's Grand Slam campaign, when he was considered to be the outstanding player in the Five Nations Championship. Leslie is first and foremost a natural footballer whose early school-ing as stand-off brought him into close contact with the basic skills and enabled him to reach a level of competence attained by few forwards. The grace of his line-out jumping, the precision of his deflections, the positioning of his body on the forward drives and his uncanny judgement of time and distance spring from a deeply rooted knowledge of the game and superb athleticism. As Leslie himself admits anyone playing the game as he does must expect to be injured now and again; he has missed more than twenty internationals as a result of injuries since winning his first cap against Ireland in 1975. Of the twenty-nine internationals in which he has played, twenty-four have been on the flank and five at number 8 where he has frequently operated for his club. He has had the rare distinction of playing for three districts – North Midlands, when he played for Dundee High School FP – Glasgow during his days at West of Scotland, and the South. He has captained the Scottish Schools, Gala to a national league title, the Scottish XV in their New Zealand tour matches against Wellington and Mid Can-terbury in 1981, and the Whites in last season's trial. Last season he moved back from Gala to his native Dundee where he works as an architect. NZ. W. E. I. F.

I A M PAXTON (Selkirk). Number 8. Born 29.12.57 in Dunfermline. 6'4". 15st 7lbs. 17 caps. Iain Paxton is something of an enigma. On the one hand he appears self-effacing and almost savagely self-critical. There is not the slightest trace of arrogance, no vaulting ambition. And yet during the Lions tour to New Zealand Paxton played in the four test matches and has twice fought back to regain his Scotland place. There is, somewhere within Paxton, a very determined young man. Last season was unquestionably his best for Scotland, his defensive awareness and positional play being so much improved. He has had to overcome the handicap of a relatively late start to rugby as a career. He was educated at Beath High in Fife and played basketball for Scottish Schools. On leaving school he joined Glenrothes, then in the seventh division of the national leagues, and when he left them to move to Selkirk in 1980 they had climbed to fourth. At Selkirk, Paxton fell under the influence of Bill Dickinson and made such good progress that he was capped the following year. An occasional lock in his early playing days, Paxton has no great wish to revert to the position although he played in the second row in the 1983 Calcutta Cup match at Twickenham and for the Scottish XV against the Barbarians that same year. An injury threatened to keep him out of the Irish game last season but he recovered in time and played his full part in Scotland's victory. His only international try to date was scored in Scotland's 15–9 win over Wales at Cardiff last season. NZ. W. E. I. F.

J R BEATTIE (Glasgow Academicals). Number 8. Born 27.11.57 in North Borneo. 6'3¾". 15st 4lbs. 14 caps. The frustrations of being on the periphery of the Scotland XV last season were most keenly felt by John Beattie who played on the flank against New Zealand and came on as a replacement lock for Bill Cuthbertson in the Calcutta Cup but, for the remainder of the season, was kept out of the side by Iain Paxton. But Beattie never lost heart and played well enough in Paxton's absence on the Rumanian tour to suggest that the rivalry between the two will, if anything, be intensified in the seasons ahead. Perhaps Beattie suffered from receiving too much too soon. He was capped at the age of twenty-two in 1980 in his first season as Glasgow's number 8 having previously played in the District under-23 side as a lock. He showed up impressively in the loose on a number of occasions during that season and although still short of experience was selected for the 1980 Lions tour of South Africa. He began promisingly but, without the benefit of proper guidance and direction, was tried as a flanker and then largely left to his own devices. He returned home, played for Scotland throughout the following season, but then missed the next eight internationals as a result of a serious knee injury. Since returning to Glasgow Academicals from Heriots, Beattie has been channelling his efforts more constructively and has been one of the major influences in Accies promotion to Division One. NZ. E(R).

Happy days are here again – Jim Telfer smiles at last

10　The Last Word

By Jim Telfer MBE

By Jim Telfer MBE

The Philosophy

On the basis that imitation is the sincerest form of flattery and that rugby is essentially a simple game, I have never made any secret of my admiration and respect for the way the game is played in New Zealand. As the years passed and I thought more and more about the game, so my conviction grew stronger that the All Blacks' style should be the one adopted by Scotland. The two countries are similar in many ways – particularly in the Borders where there are natural divides of rivers, hills and valleys, with small towns and rural communities. And it seemed to me that the style of game that was played in those rustic areas in New Zealand suited the terrain – uncompromising and unadorned.

My thoughts about the game began to crystallize in the mid-seventies and in 1978 I was asked to produce a paper entitled 'Coaching Philosophy for Scotland'. We all knew how the Springboks played their rugby and how the All Blacks played theirs but, since the forward foot rush went out of vogue, there has been nothing especially distinctive about the Scottish style of play. We tended to develop our game round the outstanding player or players of the moment, without developing a pattern. So I began to take a closer look at the characteristics of the Scottish player. I discovered that he reacts well in adversity, that he reacts well to discipline and that he is fiercely patriotic. I then looked at what I considered to be the finest aspects of New Zealand rugby and felt that they could be adapted to the Scottish temperament and environment.

Having watched All Black sides over many years, I have found that, although some have been better than others, they have all had one thing in common – an aggressive approach both in defence and attack. The players can all tackle, they can all apply pressure and they all know the shortest route to the opponents' goal line. Off the field Graham Mourie was the most mild mannered of men but put him in an All Black's jersey five yards from the try line and he was virtually unstoppable. This is the attitude of mind that I have striven to instil into the Scottish players, forwards and backs alike.

Sean McGaughey is, to my way of thinking, the most instinctively aggressive young player I have seen in Scotland since I have been involved in the game. But aggressiveness without athleticism is wasted energy. There is no place in the modern game for a forward who is embarrassed when he gets the ball in his hands. All forwards should be as proficient at handling, passing and finishing as the backs and should be taught these basic skills from the earliest age.

Unfortunately, in this country at any rate, this is seldom the case. We think too much about winning possession and too little about how to use it. But I have tried over the years to encourage and develop the all-purpose forward who can turn his hand to almost anything and be as aggressive and dynamic as the shot-putter moving across the circle. Bill Cuthbertson, for example, may not be the best scrummager in the land nor is he the ideal line-out jumper, but he can give so much elsewhere.

For all that Scotland were reputed to be a good rucking side, I consider that throughout last season the quality of our rucking was extremely variable. We rucked well against New Zealand, scattering the All Blacks like snow off a dyke for one of John Rutherford's drop goals. And we set up a classic situation against Ireland when Alister Campbell drove from a line-out and Laidlaw scored. What delighted me most about that was that the two men who rucked on Campbell – Leslie and Deans – were the two in closest support to Laidlaw when he scored. That is the essence of good rucking – being able to keep on your feet and stay in the game. I have often been described as a rucking coach and, whilst I consider it the cleanest and most effective method of winning possession, it is, like the scrum and the line-out, only a means to an end. It might even be interpreted as being an admission of failure – something which has to be done when your attack has been halted.

I have also been referred to as a man who can coach forwards but who has little idea of how to coach backs, and I would accept that. But I would like to think that, because we play to a simple formula in the forwards and because we are a rucking side, we can produce good balls for our backs to move at speed. This may be naïve, but the Australian schoolboy side of 1978 gave as near perfect a demonstration of that art as any I have seen.

There has been a bloodless revolution in New Zealand since the mid-seventies. Sid Going was a superb individualist and very much a forward's scrum-half. But by the time the 1977 Lions departed, a new breed of scrum-half was beginning to emerge in New Zealand. He was first and foremost a servant to his backs, a player who could pass off either hand. There is no place in my philosophy for ten-man rugby. Certain situations may sometimes call for a strictly limited game, but I like to see the ball moved quickly from the forwards with the backs running very straight and very hard, supported by a link-man in the Mourie

mould. I have been fortunate during my association with Scotland in having players of the calibre of Jim Calder and David Leslie in the Scottish back row. Calder is similar in so many ways to Mourie. Not so fast, perhaps, but a marvellous support player.

We were not so well equipped in the backs to play an expansive game last season. We were settled at half back but not in the mid field, largely because of injury. I am an advocate of the system of playing inside and outside centres, just as I believe that there should be a specialist open-side flanker at the tail of the line-out. To my mind there is too much responsibility placed on the stand-off who does everything nowadays except bring on the oranges at halftime. I would like to see more emphasis on mid-field play, using the inside centre as the play-maker and the stand-off as the link-man. I would go so far as to say I do not think we will improve our back play in this country until we relieve some of the pressure on the half backs. Far from making back play more stereotyped, I believe it would lead to a specialist knowledge of each position and, therefore, a general improvement in the standard of play in those positions.

I have had discussions and arguments all over the rugby world on the subject, the most recent being with the Lions in New Zealand and, having given it a great deal of thought over the years, I am certain that I am right. But, unlike my beliefs on forward play, I concede that I do not have enough success to prove my point. After devoting so much of my time to forwards as a player, captain and coach I now find an increasing interest in the challenge of back play. So much of a back's time is dissipated during a game. There is a tendency for the wings to hang around Micawber-like and they seem reluctant to go in search of hard work. The centres often give very little thought to their positions and their priorities. I remember Bruce Robertson telling me that his principal duty as a centre was to feed his wing. How many centres in this country would agree with him? And how

'Come here and say that!' The foundation of Scotland's success: Milne, Deans and Aitken.

many could execute this elementary skill with Robertson's precision? In Britain we still have so much to explore and develop regarding the full-time occupation of those players on the periphery of the action, the use of angles and the rediscovery and uses of the subtleties of back play.

Backs, unlike forwards, cannot be coached collectively; they must be treated as individuals. Our failings behind the scrum can be attributed more to indifferent coaching than to an attitude of mind amongst the players. Although I have a reputation for being a disciplinarian, I have always encouraged and welcomed free speech in the Scottish squad. Every player has had his say and, as a result, I have learned more about the game in the last four years than I did in the previous forty. Coaches are too often prepared to accept the unacceptable. I have frequently been assailed after a match by the club coach who tells me how well his side have rucked when in actual fact the word 'ruck' is a euphemism for a pile-up. It is the same in back play. We accept sluggish passing, careless handling, indisciplined running. We must insist on higher standards. As a forward I have not had any direct experience of back play and am no expert. But it is vital that we attract more imaginative thinkers into the game in order to restore British back play to its former greatness.

The Grand Slam and beyond
My feelings in the wake of Scotland's Grand Slam can quite simply be summed up in the word 'contentment'. I am not a vindictive person and therefore felt no sense of triumph over those who had been so critical of my efforts with the Lions in New Zealand. Within rugby, or any other sport, a coach or a player is only as good as his last game. There is no resting place. But for me, now, there are no ambitions left to be fulfilled as a coach and after the traumas of New Zealand there is at least peace of mind.

I have convinced myself, and I believe that I convinced Scotland, that the way we are playing our rugby at national level, particularly in the forwards, is the right way. We are a tiny rugby-playing community. We know that our resources are limited and that we must continually play above ourselves to survive. Last season I felt that, tactically, our players were very aware of the aims and knew how to achieve them. So much of that has come as a result of the mutual respect and understanding which has grown up between the players, the coach and the selectors. Without ever going so far as to suggest that democracy was rife within the squad, we did work out our problems together. The players had their own views and were encouraged to express them. Last season we talked about the game and the opposition far more

What rubbish have they given me this time? Huw Davies in a pickle and David Johnston adds to the panic in the Calcutta Cup Match

Any chance of a game, lads? Winterbottom and Scott try to break up a Scottish clique of Milne, Cuthbertson, Calder, Paxton, Leslie and Tomes

than we had done in the past. We had built up something of a family atmosphere since 1980 when we toured, in successive years, France, New Zealand and Australia. In France we discovered the need for mental and physical hardness. By the end of the New Zealand tour I considered that the players had improved by 25 per cent on their performance at the beginning. Unfortunately our domestic league structure is such that they quickly lost all that they had gained during the tour. This was frustrating because, as we showed last season, we in Scotland can produce players like Rutherford, Deans and Leslie who can hold their own in any company.

Throughout my career as a coach I have never tried to set targets and the 1983–84 season was no exception. We had not done well the previous season. We had, admittedly, beaten England at Twickenham but that was against an extremely poor English side. We had lost to Ireland at Murrayfield and had been well beaten by an experimental Welsh side. Our most convincing display had been against France in Paris; we lost the game but our forwards played far above themselves. Jim Aitken, in fact, considered it was the best game the Scots had played in his experience. But before the start of last season, I doubted that we had the consistency to win more than two games. I felt that if we did, we would be doing well as we had two hard games at home against England and France and we might suffer the backlash of our 34–18 Cardiff win in 1982.

But the draw against the All Blacks gave us great heart. We played better over a longer period in that game than we did in any other last season – although we did play well in patches in all of them. Against England we kicked accurately and we occasionally rucked well, the most obvious example being in the build-up to Euan Kennedy's try. Furthermore, we subjected the opposition to enormous pressure. We tightened our defences at Cardiff when we had to , we got off to a superb start in Dublin and we showed character against France. But I think that the psychological benefit

of the All Blacks result was enormous. We had never played against them with any great conviction that we could beat them and, although we still had not managed to break that barrier, we had come from behind to catch them. It was the launching pad for the season. My personal reaction was one of immense relief.

The saddest moment of my rugby life was when the final whistle sounded at Eden Park, Auckland, and the Lions had lost the Fourth Test 38–6. It was then that I realized that a year of hard work and three months of touring had come to nought. It was indelibly in the record books, and on my mind. I was still in a state of shock when the new season began. My greatest fear was that Scotland would lose and, to be frank, I was not sure how I would cope with another defeat against a New Zealand side. That draw, therefore, provided me with a great deal of satisfaction and, much more important, convinced me that Scotland had the appearance of a team playing together and for each other. Here were fifteen players who, individually and collectively, had decided that they were not going to be beaten. It was this blend of ability, courage and determination which enabled us to beat France later in the season.

I cannot agree that we required an unusually high degree of luck to win the Grand Slam. Certainly the Welsh made mistakes, France lost Gallion, Duggan gave us the wind and Hare missed his penalties but, as far as the latter is concerned, it merely proved that England were relying too much on one man. What was much more relevant was the timing of the Scottish scores. We always seemed to score at the right time, although the tries were not necessarily made by the right people; we didn't exactly plan, for example, that Scotland's decisive try against Wales would come from Jim Aitken. Granted, we had the breaks, but we were there to take them and we had done our homework.

I consider that the build-up to the Irish game, notwithstanding the pressure of the Triple Crown and the atrocious weather conditions, was near

That OK ref? Johnston and Paxton look to the referee for confirmation of Johnston's try against England

perfect. We were billeted 10 miles out of Dublin, we trained hard and we were genuinely confident of victory. On the Friday night we watched a video of the South's game against the All Blacks at Netherdale. There were two reasons for this. One was the positive psychological effect that I knew it would have on players like Deans, Tomes, Paxton, Laidlaw and Rutherford; the other, more important, reason was to give the players the opportunity of studying the match referee, Fred Howard, who had been in charge of that game at Netherdale. In the event, we had the wind and the kick-off, and the Irish infringed the laws more often than we did.

The French were by far the best side we met. Defensively, they were superbly well organized. Where we had found loopholes against Wales, England and Ireland, none existed against France. They frustrated us at almost every turn by holding our back row and half backs in check. It became very difficult to see how we could score a try. In the end it came from a French blunder, but it was also the result of Scottish pressure. With the exception of the Welsh game, when I think we were lucky to hold on, the players showed the positive sides of their nature. They played well within themselves, they knew what they were doing and they reaped the benefits of three years' hard labour.

As a result of this effort and Scotland's Grand Slam, I doubt that interest in the game has ever been higher in this country. How tragic it would be if it should all go to waste. The players have been lauded, so have the selectors and so have I, but we must put last season's success into perspective. We have established a formula which, in the short term at least, is a winning one. But there is no room for complacency. What we have to do now is to focus our attention on the eleven- and twelve-year-olds. As our internationalists of the future, they must receive every encouragement and the best facilities we can offer. We cannot afford to wait ten years for another Laidlaw or a Rutherford. We must never forget that Scottish rugby has to run very hard just to stand still and if people think that we start on equal terms with countries like England, Wales and France, who are so much richer in resources, they are deluding themselves. I vividly remember the occasion at the end of last season when a prominent South official commented that, apart from a hiccup against the All Blacks at Netherdale, rugby in the South of Scotland was in the best of health. If a defeat by 30 points to 9 is a hiccup I would hate to be present at a disaster. The South were destroyed that day, and yet they could still win the interdistrict title without breaking sweat.

We must obviously reappraise our domestic structure of leagues and interdistrict championships so that the best players can play against each other more often than they do at present. We may not always have the ammunition, but I am very firmly of the opinion that our players have the right attitude. We have a captive audience at present, let us not lose it through complacency or apathy. Our Grand Slam is the start – not the finish.

Appendix A

Players

Scotland v New Zealand – Murrayfield, 12 November 1983
SCOTLAND: P W Dods (Gala); J A Pollock (Gosforth), A E Kennedy (Watsonians), D I Johnston (Watsonians), G R T Baird (Kelso); J Y Rutherford (Selkirk), R J Laidlaw (Jedforest); J Aitken (Gala) capt., C T Deans (Hawick), I G Milne (Heriots FP), W Cuthbertson (Harlequins), T J Smith (Gala), J H Calder (Stewarts Melville FP), J R Beattie (Glasgow Academicals), I A M Paxton (Selkirk).

NEW ZEALAND: R M Deans (Canterbury); S S Wilson (Wellington) capt., S T Pokere (Southland), W T Taylor (Canterbury), B G Fraser (Wellington); W R Smith (Canterbury), A J Donald (Wanganui); B McGrattan (Wellington), H R Reid (Bay of Plenty), S A Crichton (Wellington), G J Braid (Bay of Plenty), A Anderson (Canterbury), M W Shaw (Manawatu), M J B Hobbs (Canterbury), M G Mexted (Wellington).

Referee: R Hourquet (France).

Scotland v Wales – National Stadium, Cardiff, 21 January 1984
SCOTLAND: P W Dods (Gala); S Munro (Ayr), D I Johnston (Watsonians), A E Kennedy (Watsonians), G R T Baird (Kelso); J Y Rutherford (Selkirk), R J Laidlaw (Jedforest); J Aitken (Gala) capt., C T Deans (Hawick), I G Milne (Heriots FP), W Cuthbertson (Harlequins), A J Tomes (Hawick), J H Calder (Stewarts Melville FP), D G Leslie (Gala), I A M Paxton (Selkirk).

WALES: H Davies (Bridgend); M H Titley (Bridgend), R A Ackerman (London Welsh), B Bowen (South Wales Police), A M Hadley (Cardiff); M Dacey (Swansea), M H J Douglas (Llanelli); S T Jones (Pontypool), W J James (Aberavon), R Morgan (Newport), S J Perkins (Pontypool), R L Norster (Cardiff), R D Moriarty (Swansea), D F Pickering (Llanelli), E T Butler (Pontypool) capt.

Referee: O Doyle (Ireland)

Scotland v England – Murrayfield, 4 February 1984
SCOTLAND: P W Dods (Gala); K W Robertson (Melrose), D I Johnston (Watsonians), A E Kennedy (Watsonians), G R T Baird (Kelso); J Y Rutherford (Selkirk), R J Laidlaw (Jedforest); J Aitken (Gala) capt., C T Deans (Hawick), I G Milne (Heriots FP), W Cuthbertson (Harlequins), A J Tomes (Hawick), J H Calder (Stewarts Melville FP), D G Leslie (Gala), I A M Paxton (Selkirk).
Replacements: J R Beattie (Glasgow Academicals) for Cuthbertson; J A Pollock (Gosforth) for Kennedy.

ENGLAND: W H Hare (Leicester); J Carleton (Orrell), C R Woodward (Leicester), G H Davies (Wasps), M A C Slemen (Liverpool); L Cusworth (Leicester), N G Youngs (Leicester), C White (Gosforth), P J Wheeler (Leicester) capt., G S Pearce (Northampton), M J Colclough (Wasps), S J Bainbridge (Gosforth), P D Simpson (Bath), P J Winterbottom (Headingley), J P

Scott (Cardiff).
Replacement: J Hall (Bath) for Winterbottom.

Referee: D I H Burnett (Ireland).

Scotland v Ireland – Lansdowne Road, 3 March 1984
SCOTLAND: P W Dods (Gala); J A Pollock (Gosforth), K W Robertson (Melrose), D I Johnston (Watsonians), G R T Baird (Kelso); J Y Rutherford (Selkirk), R J Laidlaw (Jedforest); J Aitken (Gala) capt., C T Deans (Hawick), I G Milne (Heriots FP), A J Campbell (Hawick), A J Tomes (Hawick), J H Calder (Stewarts Melville FP), D G Leslie (Gala), I A M Paxton (Selkirk).
Replacements: I G Hunter (Selkirk) for Laidlaw.

IRELAND: J J Murphy (Greystones); T Ringland (Ballymena), M J Kiernan (Lansdowne), M C Finn (Cork Constitution), K D Crossan (Instonians); A J P Ward (St Mary's College), J A P Doyle (Greystones); P A Orr (Old Wesley), H T Harbison (Bective Rangers), D C Fitzgerald (Lansdowne), M I Keane (Lansdowne), D G Lenihan (Cork Constitution), J B O'Driscoll (London Irish), D G McGrath (U.C.D.), W P Duggan (Blackrock College) capt.
Replacement: H C Condon (London Irish) for Ward.

Referee: F A Howard (England).

Scotland v France – Murrayfield, 17 March 1984
SCOTLAND: P W Dods (Gala); J A Pollock (Gosforth), K W Robertson (Melrose), D I Johnston (Watsonians), G R T Baird (Kelso); J Y Rutherford (Selkirk), R J Laidlaw (Jedforest); J Aitken (Gala) capt., C T Deans (Hawick), I G Milne (Heriots FP), A J Campbell (Hawick), A J Tomes (Hawick), J H Calder (Stewarts Melville FP), D G Leslie (Gala), I A M Paxton (Selkirk).

FRANCE: S Blanco (Biarritz); J Bégu (Dax), P Sella (Agen), D Codorniou (Narbonne), P Estève (Narbonne); J P Lescarboura (Dax), J Gallion (Toulon); P Dospital (Bayonne), P Dintrans (Tarbes), D Dubroca (Agen), F Haget (Biarritz), J Condom (Boucau), J P Rives (Racing Club de France) capt., J L Joinel (Brive), J C Orso (Nice).
Replacement: P Berbizier (Lourdes) for Gallion.

Referee: W Jones (Wales).

Appendix B

The Scorers

	T	P	C	DG	PTS
v New Zealand					
P W Dods		5			15
J Y Rutherford				2	6
J A Pollock	1				4
v Wales					
P W Dods		1	2		7
I A M Paxton	1				4
J Aitken	1				4
v England					
P W Dods		2	2		10
D I Johnston	1				4
A E Kennedy	1				4
v Ireland					
P W Dods	1	2	3		16
R J Laidlaw	2				8
K W Robertson	1				4
Penalty Try	1				4
v France					
P W Dods		5	1		17
J H Calder	1				4